Creative
Log Cabin
Quilting™

EDITED BY JEANNE STAUFFER AND SANDRA L. HATCH

HOUSE of
WHITE
BIRCHES

PUBLISHERS
SINCE 1947

CREATIVE LOG CABIN QUILTING

EDITORS	Jeanne Stauffer, Sandra L. Hatch
ASSOCIATE EDITOR	Dianne Schmidt
COPY EDITORS	Sue Harvey, Nicki Lehman, Mary Martin
PHOTOGRAPHY	Tammy Christian, Kelly Heydinger, Christena Green
PHOTO STYLIST	Tammy Nussbaum
ART DIRECTOR	Brad Snow
PRODUCTION MANAGER	Brenda Gallmeyer
GRAPHIC ARTS SUPERVISOR	Ronda Bechinski
GRAPHIC ARTIST	Amy S. Lin
PRODUCTION ASSISTANT	Marj Morgan
TECHNICAL ARTIST	Connie Rand
CHIEF EXECUTIVE OFFICER	John Robinson
PUBLISHING DIRECTOR	David J. McKee
BOOK MARKETING DIRECTOR	Craig Scott
EDITORIAL DIRECTOR	Vivian Rothe

Printed in the United States of America
First Printing: 2004
Library of Congress Number: 2004103266
ISBN: 1-59217-037-4

Welcome

You'll love creating Log Cabin quilts today. They're quick, they're easy and they're fun to make. They are also very different from the Log Cabin quilts your grandmother made.

Some Log Cabin designs use the traditional rectangular strips added around a square center. Other designs start with a center that is anything but square. The added strips are not just rectangles, but triangles and crazy shapes that create Log Cabin quilts that are unique and very up-to-date. Traditionally, Log Cabin quilts were created using a fabric foundation. The same is true today, only now the foundation can be paper, lightweight interfacing or fabric.

Whether you like quilts that provide a nostalgic glimpse of yesteryear or unconventional designs that are highly unique, we're sure you'll agree that this collection of Log Cabin quilts is spectacular!

So, welcome to *Creative Log Cabin Quilting.* Come in and enjoy the fun activity of deciding which quilt to stitch first. It won't be long before you're deciding on the second quilt to stitch, then the third, the fourth and so on. You'll be surprised how quickly you can make a Log Cabin quilt. And you'll enjoy every stitch!

Warm regards,

Jeanne Stauffer

Sandra L. Hatch

Contents

Found-ation

View

Walls

Home

Laying the **Foundation**

Building the **Walls**

Adding a **View**

Making It **Home**

General Instructions for Paper or Foundation Piecing

Paper- or fabric-foundation pieces are used to make very accurate blocks, provide stability for weak fabrics, and add body and weight to the finished quilt.

Temporary-foundation materials include paper, tracing paper, freezer paper and removable interfacing or stabilizer. Permanent foundations include utility fabrics, nonwoven interfacing, flannel, fleece and batting. Piecing on a foundation results in complete accuracy. Quilters usually use this method when piecing with very small pieces or when stitching a complicated pieced unit or block.

Log Cabin designs may be pieced on a foundation. Even the most basic designs may be pieced in this method, if a quilter prefers it to other methods.

Many patterns in this book recommend using paper foundations. The instructions for these projects direct you to make a certain number of copies of the provided pattern. You may choose freezer paper or typing paper or even fabric as foundations.

The patterns provided for foundation piecing have been reversed. Because you stitch on the marked side of the paper, but the opposite side is the finished fabric right side, the pattern must be reversed.

Begin by making the copies as directed. Methods of marking foundations include basting lines, pencils or pens, needlepunching, tracing wheel, hot-iron transfers, copy machine, computer printed, premarked, stamps or stencils. Copy patterns given here using a copy machine or trace each block individually. **(Photo 1)** Measure the finished paper foundations to insure accuracy in copying.

There are two methods of foundation piecing—under piecing and top piecing. When under piecing, the pattern is reversed when tracing. We have not included any patterns for top piecing. Although some patterns recommend stitching strips to a muslin foundation, this is not the same as a marked foundation that is pieced from the marked side for top piecing. In the case of using muslin, it is used as a stabilizer and is not marked. **Note:** *All patterns for which we recommend paper piecing are already reversed in full-size drawings given.*

To under piece, place a scrap of fabric larger than the lined space on the unmarked side of the paper or foundation material in the No. 1 position. **(Photo 2)**

3

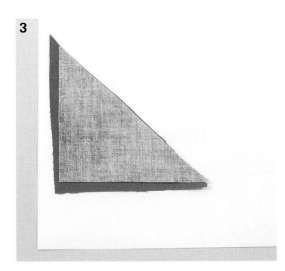

5a

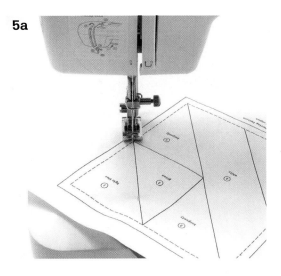

4a

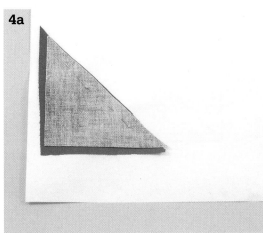

5b

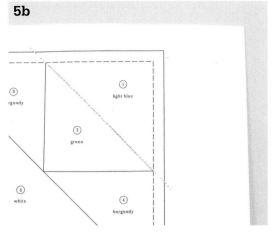

4b

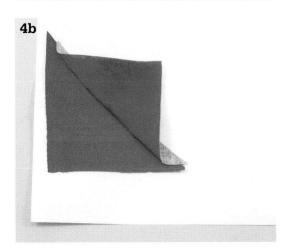

6

Place piece 2 right sides together with piece 1. **(Photo 3)** Pin on seam line and fold back to check that the piece will cover space 2 before stitching. **(Photo 4a and 4b)**

Use a smaller stitch than for normal sewing—12–14 stitches per inch or 2mm to allow for ease in removing foundation

later. Stitch along line on the lined side of the paper—fabric will not be visible. Sew several stitches beyond the beginning and end of the line. **(Photos 5a and 5b)** Backstitching is not required, as another fabric seam will cover this seam. Trim seam to ⅛". **(Photo 6)**

7

8b

8a

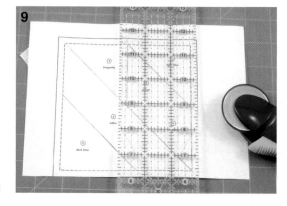

9

Remove pin; finger-press piece 2 flat. **(Photo 7)** Continue adding all pieces in numerical order in the same manner until all pieces are stitched to paper. **(Photo 8a and 8b)** Trim excess to outside line (¼" larger all around than finished size of the block). **(Photo 9)**

Temporary-foundation materials are removed when blocks are complete and stitched together or as directed in the patterns. Permanent foundations remain on

the wrong side of the blocks and become part of the quilt. They add another layer and increase bulk.

Tip

To help with placement on the wrong side of the foundation, prefold on the marked lines. You may also stitch on the lines with an unthreaded sewing machine set on a larger stitch to mark the lines. 🏠

Completed block front side

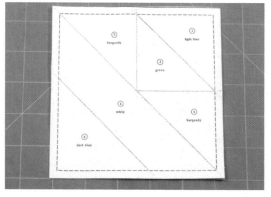

Completed block back side

General Instructions for the Log Cabin Method

Piecing Log Cabin blocks is fun. Piecing multiple blocks at one time speeds up the process and eliminates wasted time and fabric. Adding the first round of strips around the center square doesn't take much time and gives a feeling of accomplishment right away. As the sides get longer, the stitching takes longer and those last few logs require lots of fabric and more time. By that time, you are hooked and can't wait to see the finished results.

Most quilters have made at least one Log Cabin quilt in their quilting lifetimes. This pattern is one of the all-time favorites for quilters. Over time, fast-piecing techniques have replaced some of the traditional methods, and quilters find solace in the repetitious stitching, pressing and cutting techniques required for making the blocks.

When working with the patterns in this book, you will be instructed to refer to these instructions frequently rather than repeat the same instructions with each pattern. Once you have discovered the simplicity of traditional patterns, you will want to try some of the more difficult designs. These patterns use the same methods, but the sizes of the strips, shapes in the center or other variables occur.

TRADITIONAL LOG CABIN METHOD

In the traditional Log Cabin block, the rounds around the center are added to adjacent sides in numerical order as shown in **Figure 1**.

Traditional Log Cabin blocks can be pieced in several ways. The traditional method includes making templates and cutting exact-size pieces for each log. This is a time-consuming way to piece Log Cabin blocks and is rarely used today. If pieces are cut to the exact size, they are more apt to be cut from the correct-size strips in the increments needed. For example, if a Log Cabin strip finishes at 1" x 6", a 1½"-wide strip is cut into 6½" lengths, or a 6½"-wide strip is cut into 1½" lengths as shown in **Figure 2**.

One step in the above process may be eliminated by cutting the correct-width strips and chain-sewing. For this method, you begin with the block center cut to the correct size. For example, a 2" finished center begins with a 2½" cut square. Cut the correct number of 2½"-wide strips; then subcut the strips into 2½" segments.

These center squares, or No. 1 pieces, are then stitched to a strip of fabric for the first log or the No. 2 piece as shown in **Figure 3**. Once

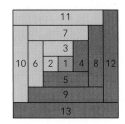

FIGURE 1 In the traditional Log Cabin method, the rounds are added around the center in numerical order.

FIGURE 2 Strips may be cut in 2 ways.

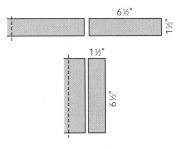

FIGURE 3 Stitch the No. 1 piece to the No. 2 strip.

all the No. 1 center squares are stitched to the strip, the strip is trimmed even with the No. 1 pieces as shown in **Figure 4**. This may be done before or after pressing. If trimmed before pressing, each cut unit must be pressed with the seam facing the No. 2 strip. If pressing before trimming, carefully press the entire seam toward the strip and then trim as shown in **Figure 5**.

Additional strips are added in numerical order placing the stitched unit on the strip, keeping the last-added strip facing you on the strip as shown in **Figure 6**.

During this process, the size of the stitched unit should be checked several times. Inaccurate stitching can result in finished blocks that are either not square or not a consistent size. It helps to check the size when half the strips have been added around the center square. If the size is not accurate, it helps to trim the blocks to size at this time.

Another timesaving method works when the center and the first log strips are stitched together and subcut into the correct size. These two pieces are cut from a pieced strip to eliminate cutting the center square to size. For example, using the above sizes, a 2" finished No. 1 center square is bordered by 1" finished logs. For this example, cut a 2½" by fabric width strip from the center square fabric and a 1½" by fabric width strip of the No. 2 log fabric.

Join these strips with right sides together along length; press seams toward the No. 2 strip. Subcut the pieced strip into 2½" segments as shown in **Figure 7** to complete stitching of the first two pieces of the block. Continue adding consecutive strips in the same manner as before.

COURTHOUSE STEPS METHOD

When making Courthouse Steps blocks, the logs are added to opposite sides of the center instead of to adjacent sides as shown in **Figure 8**.

The blocks begin with a center square with a strip added to one side and then the opposite side. As in traditional methods, you may begin with templates or strips, but the easiest way to begin is with strips.

For example, using a 2" finished No. 1 center square and 1" finished strips, cut one 2½" by fabric width strip of the center fabric and two 1½" by fabric width strips of the No. 2 and No. 3 fabrics. Sew No. 2 and No. 3 fabric strips to opposite sides of the No. 1 strip with right sides together along length; press seams away from the No. 1 strip. Subcut the strip set into 2½" segments to complete the block center with two rounds as shown in **Figure 9**.

Continue to add strips to opposite sides of the center in numerical order as for traditional blocks to complete multiple blocks at one time.

FIGURE 4 Trim the strip even with the No. 1 pieces.

FIGURE 6 The last-added strip faces you on the strip.

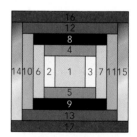

FIGURE 8 In the Courthouse Steps block, the logs are added to opposite sides of the center.

FIGURE 5 Press and then trim the strip even with the No. 1 pieces.

FIGURE 7 Subcut the pieced strip into 2½" segments.

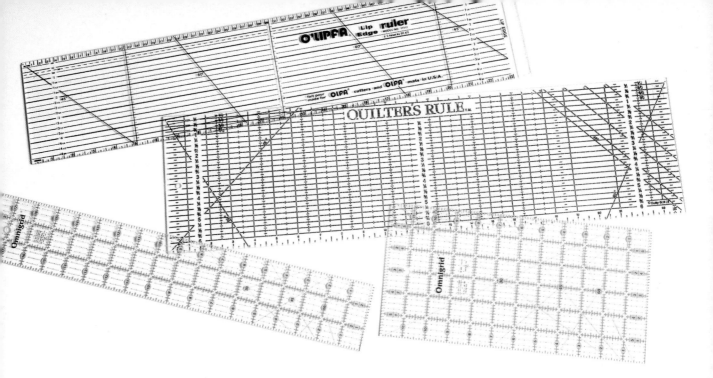

UNUSUAL BLOCKS

Sometimes the center shape varies. It might be a triangle or a diamond. In this case, the resulting block may not be called a Log Cabin block, but it uses the same methods.

Begin with the center or No. 1 piece. It can be cut in the correct-width strip and then subcut into the right shape, either with a ruler or template as shown in **Figure 10**.

After that initial cut, the No. 1 piece is stitched to the No. 2 strip as in the traditional method and pressed. The resulting stitched strip is then subcut into the correct shape using an angled ruler as shown in **Figure 11**.

This type of block is a little more complicated and harder to complete, but with the right tools, accuracy is assured, and blocks may be completed quickly. Look for rulers with 45- and 60-degree angles, such as those in the photo at the top of the page.

TIMESAVING HINT

Cut the fabric-width strips of one fabric and join all of them on the short ends into one long strip. This eliminates leftover parts of strips and makes it possible to stitch all the blocks at once. 🏠

FIGURE 9 Subcut the strip set into 2½" segments to complete the block center with 2 rounds.

FIGURE 10 Subcut strip into the right shape, either with a ruler or template.

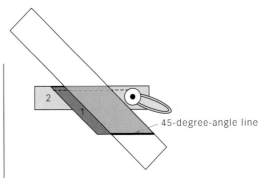

FIGURE 11 Subcut the stitched strips into the correct shape using an angled ruler.

The fabric foundation of early Log Cabin quilts reflected the sturdiness of pioneer cabins. Common choices for foundations today are muslin, interfacing and paper.

Laying the Foundation

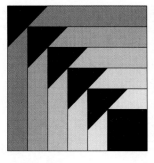

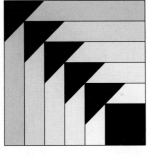

SHADOWS
5¼" x 5¼" Block

SUNSHINE
5¼" x 5¼" Block

DESIGN > CONNIE KAUFFMAN

Sunshine & Shadows

Fat quarters of hand-dyed fabrics combine with black solid to make a striking wall quilt.

PROJECT SPECIFICATIONS

Skill Level: Intermediate
Quilt Size: 31½" x 31½"
Block Size: 5¼" x 5¼"
Number of Blocks: 36

MATERIALS

- 5 fat quarters of hand-dyed yellows from light to dark shades
- 5 fat quarters hand-dyed greens from light to dark shades
- 1 yard black solid
- Backing 38" x 38"
- Batting 38" x 38"
- Neutral color all-purpose thread
- Quilting thread
- Clear nylon monofilament
- Basic sewing tools and supplies

INSTRUCTIONS

Step 1. Make 36 copies of the paper-piecing pattern given.

Step 2. Label green fabrics from 1–5 with 5 being the darkest color. Cut the following 1¼" x 18" strips from the green fabrics: 17 strips green 5; 13 strips green 4; 11 strips green 3; nine strips green 2 and seven strips green 1.

Note: *If your fabric is not cut a true 18" x 22" fat quarter, you may have a problem cutting 17 strips of the darkest fabric; 16 strips will work, but you must not waste any.*

Step 3. Label yellow fabrics from 1–5 with 5 being the darkest color. Cut the following 1¼" x 18" strips from the yellow fabrics: nine strips yellow 5; seven strips yellow 4; six strips yellow 3; five strips yellow 2 and four strips yellow 1.

Step 4. Cut two strips black solid 2" by fabric width; subcut strips into 2" square segments. You will need 36 squares for piece 1 in each block.

Step 5. Cut six strips black solid 2⅜" by fabric width; subcut into 2⅜" square segments. Cut each square in half on one diagonal to make 180 black solid triangles.

Step 6. Referring to the instructions given on page 6–8 for foundation piecing, complete 24 blocks with green fabrics and 12 blocks with yellow fabrics using the paper foundation copies made in Step 1 and starting with the lightest fabric strips to the darkest fabric strips referring to **Figure 1**.

Step 7. When all blocks are complete, arrange in six rows of six blocks each referring to **Figure 2**. Join blocks in rows; press seams in one direction. Join rows; press. Remove paper foundations.

Finishing the Quilt

Step 1. Prepare quilt top for quilting and quilt.

Step 2. When quilting is complete, trim batting and backing edges even with quilted top.

Step 3. Prepare 4 yards black solid binding and bind edges of quilt to finish.

SUNSHINE & SHADOWS Placement Diagram 31½" x 31½"

Make 24

Make 12

FIGURE 1 Make yellow and green blocks in the order shown.

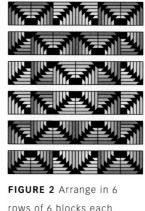

FIGURE 2 Arrange in 6 rows of 6 blocks each.

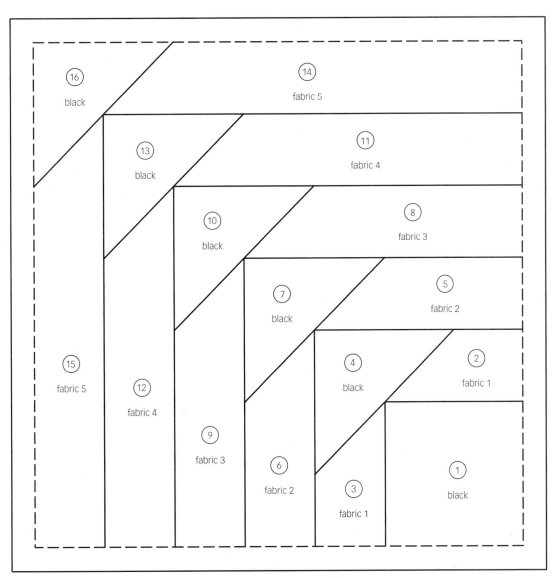

PAPER-PIECING PATTERN

Make 36 copies

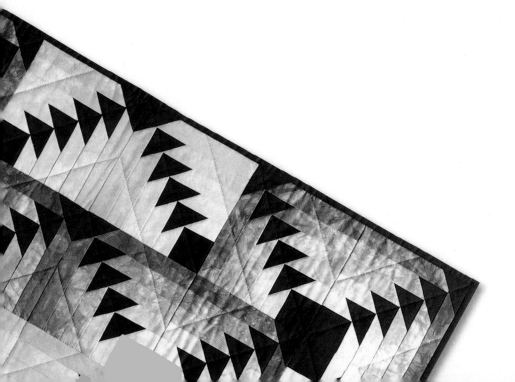

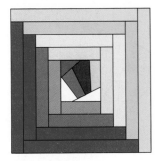

CRAZY-PATCH LOG
14" x 14" Block

Crazy-Patch Log

Make the center squares stand out by completing crazy-patchwork centers on a batting foundation.

PROJECT SPECIFICATIONS

Skill Level: Intermediate

Quilt Size: 94" x 94"

Block Size: 14" x 14"

Number of Blocks: 24

MATERIALS

- ⅛ yard each black-with-white 1 and white-with-black 1 prints
- ⅛ yard yellow/black/white print
- ⅓ yard black-with-white print 2
- ⅜ yard red print 1
- ⅝ yard white-with-black print 2
- ⅝ yard each yellow print 1 and red print 2
- ⅔ yard yellow print 2
- ¾ yard red print 3
- ⅞ yard yellow print 3
- 1 yard black solid
- 1⅛ yards yellow print 4
- 1¼ yards yellow dot
- 1⅓ yards red print 4
- 2¾ yards red/black/white print
- Backing 100" x 100"
- Batting 100" x 100"
- 24 squares batting 5" x 5"

- Neutral color all-purpose thread
- Quilting thread
- Basic sewing tools and supplies

PROJECT NOTES

The fabrics do not have to be used in the same round on each block as long as the yellow is on one side and the red is on the other. If the fabrics are similar in value, they may be stitched in any order. It does help to have the last strip in both fabrics the same.

In the sample quilt, two of the red fabrics were switched from the first round and third round because of fabric limitations. This made it possible to make the quilt without purchasing another fabric. This does not show in the overall quilt and is not easy to find upon inspection. Can you find the switch?

Choose the order of color piecing and label the first red strip as red print 1 and the first yellow strip as yellow print 1. Consecutive fabrics are numbered 2, 3 and 4 of each color.

INSTRUCTIONS

Step 1. Cut two 4½" x 86½" F strips and two

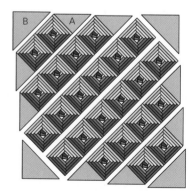

4½" x 94½" G strips red/black/white print along the length of the fabric; set aside for borders.

Step 2. To make crazy-patch centers for the Log Cabin blocks, cut small pieces of red/black/white, yellow/black/white and each of the black and white prints.

Step 3. Center a colored scrap on one 5" x 5" square of batting; pin to hold. Pin and stitch a scrap of black or white print right sides together with the pinned No. 1 center scrap as shown in **Figure 1**; stitch. Finger-press the No. 2 piece flat, again referring to **Figure 1**.

Step 4. Repeat on the opposite side of the No. 1 piece with a second black or white scrap. Continue adding scrap pieces until the entire batting square is covered as shown in **Figure 2**. Repeat for 24 crazy-patch centers.

Step 5. Trim all crazy-patch centers to 4½" x 4½".

Step 6. Cut the following 1¾" by fabric width strips: six strips red 1 for pieces 1 and 2; eight strips yellow 1 for pieces 3 and 4; nine strips red 2 for pieces 5 and 6; 11 strips yellow 2 for pieces 7 and 8; 12 strips red 3 for pieces 9 and 10; 15 strips yellow 3 for pieces 11 and 12; 16 strips red 4 for pieces 13 and 14; and 20 strips yellow 4 for pieces 15 and 16. **Note:** *If joining strips on short ends to make one long strip, you may reduce the number of strips needed and eliminate some waste.*

Step 7. Beginning with red print 1 strips, add the consecutive rounds around the crazy-patch center square referring to **Figure 3** for order of placement and to page 9–11 for making Log Cabin blocks.

Step 8. Complete 24 blocks; measure and trim to 14½" x 14½".

Step 9. Cut two 21" x 21" squares yellow dot for A. Cut each square on both diagonals as shown in **Figure 4** to make A side triangles.

Step 10. Cut two 20⅝" x 20⅝" squares yellow dot for B. Cut each square on one diagonal to make B corner triangles, again referring to **Figure 4**.

Step 11. Arrange the blocks in diagonal rows with A and B triangles as shown in **Figure 5**. Join to make rows; press seams in one direction. Join rows and add B to opposite corners to complete the pieced center; press seams in one direction.

Step 12. Cut and piece two 2" x 79½" C strips and two 2" x 82½" D strips red print 4. Sew C to opposite sides and D to the top and bottom of

FIGURE 1 Place a black or white scrap right sides together with pinned No. 1 scrap; stitch and finger-press No. 2 flat.

FIGURE 2 Add scrap pieces to cover the batting square.

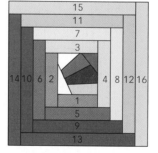

FIGURE 3 Piece blocks in numerical order as shown.

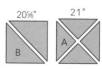

FIGURE 4 Cut squares as shown to make A and B triangles.

FIGURE 5 Join the blocks in diagonal rows with A and B triangles.

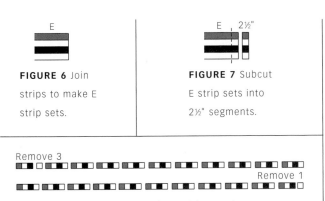

the pieced center; press seams toward strips.

Step 13. Cut three strips each 2½" by fabric width black solid and black-and-white print 2 and six strips 2½" by fabric width white-with-black print 2. Join two white-with-black print 2 strips with one black solid and one black-with-white print 2 strip with right sides together along length to make a strip set as shown in **Figure 6**; press seams toward darker strips. Repeat for three strip sets.

Step 14. Subcut strip sets into 2½" E segments as shown in **Figure 7**.

Step 15. Join 11 E segments on short ends to make one long strip; repeat for four strips and press.

Step 16. Remove three segments from one end of two strips as shown in **Figure 8**; sew one of these strips to opposite sides of the pieced center. Press seams away from the E strips.

Step 17. Remove one segment from the end of the remaining two strips, again referring to **Figure 8**. Sew these strips to the top and bottom of the pieced center.

Step 18. Sew the previously cut F strips to opposite sides and the G strips to the top and bottom of the pieced center to complete the top; press seams toward F and G.

Finishing the Quilt

Step 1. Prepare quilt top for quilting and quilt.

Step 2. When quilting is complete, trim batting and backing edges even with quilted top.

Step 3. Prepare 10¾ yards black solid binding and bind edges of quilt to finish. 🏠

CRAZY-PATCH LOG Placement Diagram 94" x 94"

COLOR KEY

- ■ Black-with-white print 1
- ■ Black-with-white print 2
- ■ Black solid
- □ White-with-black print 1
- □ White-with-black print 2
- ■ Yellow/black/white print 1
- ■ Yellow print 1
- ■ Yellow print 2
- ■ Yellow print 3
- ■ Yellow print 4
- ■ Yellow dot
- ■ Red/black/white print
- ■ Red print 1
- ■ Red print 2
- ■ Red print 3
- ■ Red print 4

E

FIGURE 6 Join strips to make E strip sets.

E   2½"

FIGURE 7 Subcut E strip sets into 2½" segments.

Remove 3

Remove 1

FIGURE 8 Remove segments from strips as shown.

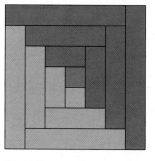

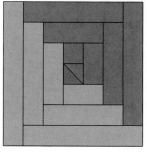

SQUARE CENTER LOG CABIN
1¾" x 1¾" Block

SPLIT CENTER LOG CABIN
1¾" x 1¾" Block

Mini Log Cabin
Heart

Tiny ¼"-wide finished strips make up the blocks that create the heart design in this mini Log Cabin design.

PROJECT SPECIFICATIONS

Skill Level: Intermediate

Quilt Size: 11½" x 11½" (includes binding)

Block Size: 1¾" x 1¾"

Number of Blocks: 16

MATERIALS

- ¼ yard each 6 different lavender/blue solids
- ¼ yard black print
- ¼ yard blue print
- 5" x 5" scrap hot pink solid
- ⅞" x 32" strip aqua solid
- Backing 14" x 14"
- Thin cotton batting 14" x 14"
- Neutral color all-purpose thread
- Quilting thread
- Glue stick
- ¼"-ruled graph paper with lines on front and back
- Basic sewing tools and supplies, seam ripper and tweezers

PROJECT NOTES

When choosing fabrics, select solids or small prints for the heart design, graduating in color either from light to dark or from one color family to the other, for example, pinks through purples. You will need six colors for the heart itself, one for the background A fabric, which should be a neutral color, and a completely different fabric for the center of each square—this should be a zinger fabric. The sample uses hand-dyed fabrics in purples and blues for the heart, with hot pink centers. The background is a dark-color print to highlight the solids used to make the heart shape.

INSTRUCTIONS

Making Blocks

Step 1. Cut the four different lavender/blue solids into ⅞" by fabric width strips; label fabrics B–G. **Note:** *These strips are cut wider than needed to complete ¼"-finished strips, but when using the paper-foundation method, this does not matter.*

Step 2. Cut 14 squares hot pink solid and 10 squares black print ⅞" x ⅞" for H center squares or triangle/squares.

Step 3. Cut sixteen 2¼" x 2¼" squares ¼"-ruled graph paper. **Note:** *Each square should be nine squares by nine squares of graph paper.*

Step 4. Using the glue stick, glue a hot pink solid H square right side up to the center of the graph-paper square, centering it over the middle square as shown in **Figure 1**.

FIGURE 1 Center and glue an H square over the middle square on the graph paper.

FIGURE 3 Make center triangle/square as shown.

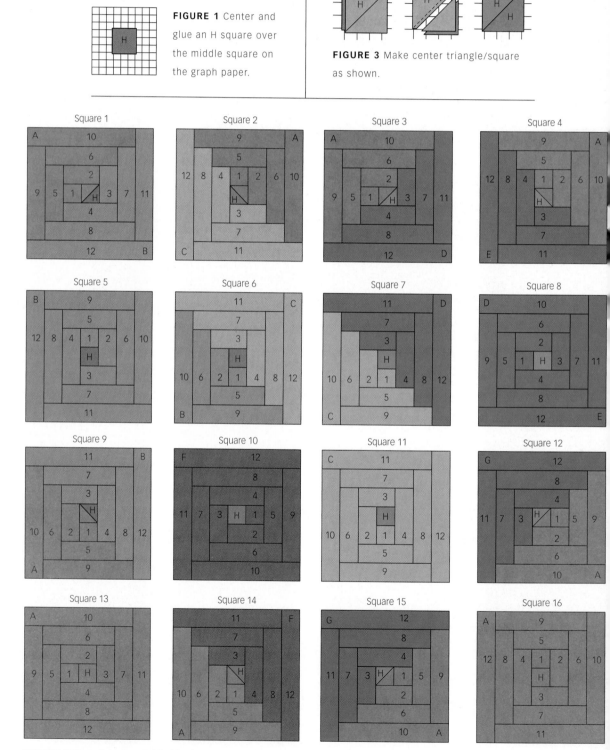

FIGURE 2 Complete Log Cabin blocks referring to numbers and colors for each block.

The width of the blocks is almost the same as that of an ordinary pencil.

Step 5. To piece Square 5, place a B strip right sides together with a hot pink solid H, cutting B to match the length of the square, edges meeting (they should not reach the next line on the graph paper); pin in place. Flip the paper over and sew exactly on the graph-paper line, sewing a few stitches past ends of fabric on both ends. Trim seams to a scant ¼" after stitching. **Note:** *You will cut all pieces as you go along to match the length of the piece you are sewing to.*

Step 6. Flip paper over and finger-press seam flat. Continue adding strips in numerical and color order referring to **Figure 2** for all blocks. Repeat for blocks 5, 6, 7, 8, 10 and 11 using hot pink solid H squares in the center and blocks 13 and 16 using black print H squares in the center.

Step 7. Draw a diagonal line from corner to corner on the wrong side of the remaining black print H squares.

Step 8. Referring to Step 4, place a hot pink solid H square in the center of a graph-paper square. Place a black print H square right

sides together with the hot pink square and stitch on the drawn line to make a triangle/ square center as shown in **Figure 3**; trim seam to a scant ¼".

Step 9. Complete blocks 1, 2, 3, 4, 9, 12, 14 and 15, again referring to **Figure 2** for color and order of adding strips.

Step 10. Trim all blocks even with graph-paper foundations.

Completing the Top

Step 1. When all blocks are complete, lay out in rows referring to **Figure 2** and the Placement Diagram; join blocks in rows, stitching along graph-paper lines. Finger-press seams in one direction.

Step 2. Join the rows to complete the pieced center; finger-press seams in one direction.

Step 3. Cut two strips graph paper 32 squares by three squares and two strips 30 squares by three squares.

Step 4. Cut two ⅞" x 7½" I strips and two ⅞" x 8" J strips aqua solid.

Step 5. Position an I strip on the 30 squares

by three squares graph-paper strip, centering the paper strip on the wrong side of the I strip; baste along center of the layered strips, not on the sewing line, to secure.

Step 6. Center the basted I strip along the top edge of the pieced center with right sides together. Pin and sew along the ¼" sewing line on the graph paper. Flip the paper and strip to the right side, press. Repeat on the bottom; trim seams to a scant ¼". Trim edges even with graph-paper foundations; remove basting.

Step 7. Repeat with the J strips and the 32 squares by three squares graph-paper strips and sew to the remaining sides of the pieced center. Press and trim as in Step 6.

Step 8. Cut two 2½" x 8" K and two 2½" x 12" L strips blue print. Sew K to opposite sides and L to the top and bottom; press seams toward strips. Measure and square up the whole piece to 11½" x 11½".

Step 9. Remove paper using a seam ripper and small tweezers.

Finishing the Quilt

Step 1. Prepare quilt top for quilting and quilt.

Step 2. When quilting is complete, trim batting and backing edges even with quilted top.

Step 3. Prepare 1½ yards black print binding and bind edges of quilt to finish.

Mounting the Finished Quilt

MATERIALS

- 16" x 16" square 5mm clear acrylic plastic
- Picture wire
- Tape
- Fine-tip permanent marker
- ⅛" drill bit and drill
- Black thread and hand-sewing needle

INSTRUCTIONS

Step 1. Using a fine-tip permanent marker, mark the location of holes to be drilled on the acrylic plastic square. On the sample there are 10 holes as shown in **Figure 4**.

Step 2. After drilling the holes, attach picture wire in the two center holes, tape the quilt in position on top of the acrylic plastic to secure and hand-stitch the quilt to the frame through the holes using matching thread; do not allow stitches to come through to the front side of the quilt. Remove tape. 🏠

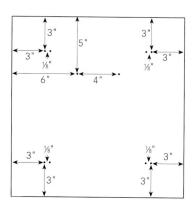

FIGURE 4 Mark the acrylic plastic square as shown.

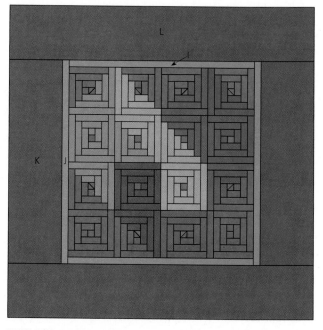

MINI LOG CABIN HEART Placement Diagram 11½" x 11½" (includes binding)

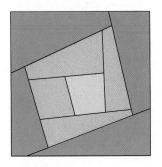

CRAZY LOG
5" x 5" Block

Crazy Logs
Kid's Quilt

Off-center Log Cabin blocks, using an assortment of bright, colorful children's prints, give this quilt a true scrappy look.

PROJECT SPECIFICATIONS

Skill Level: Beginner
Quilt Size: 40½" x 46¾"
Block Size: 5" x 5"
Number of Blocks: 30

MATERIALS

- Fat quarters of 15–20 bright prints
- ⅙ yard yellow tone-on-tone
- ⅓ yard aqua mottled
- ½ yard yellow stripe for binding
- ½ yard white-on-white print
- Backing 47" x 53"
- Batting 47" x 53"
- Neutral color all-purpose thread
- Quilting thread
- Basic sewing tools and supplies

INSTRUCTIONS

Making Blocks

Step 1. Cut 30 squares yellow tone-on-tone 2" x 2" for block centers.

Step 2. Cut four 2" x 18" and four 2¾" x 18" strips from each bright print.

Step 3. Make 30 copies of the Crazy Log paper-piecing pattern. Pre-fold all lines on each pattern.

Step 4. Pin a 2" x 2" yellow tone-on-tone square right side up on the unmarked side of one paper pattern, covering the center No. 1 space.

Step 5. Choose one 2" x 18" strip bright print for pieces 2, 3, 4 and 5. Pin the strip right sides together with piece 1; turn paper over and stitch on the marked line between pieces 1 and 2. **Note:** *The fabric strips will be underneath the paper.*

Step 6. Turn paper over; press piece 2 flat and trim excess strip beyond the line between pieces 2 and 3 as shown in **Figure 1**.

FIGURE 1 Press piece 2 flat and trim excess strip beyond the line between pieces 2 and 3.

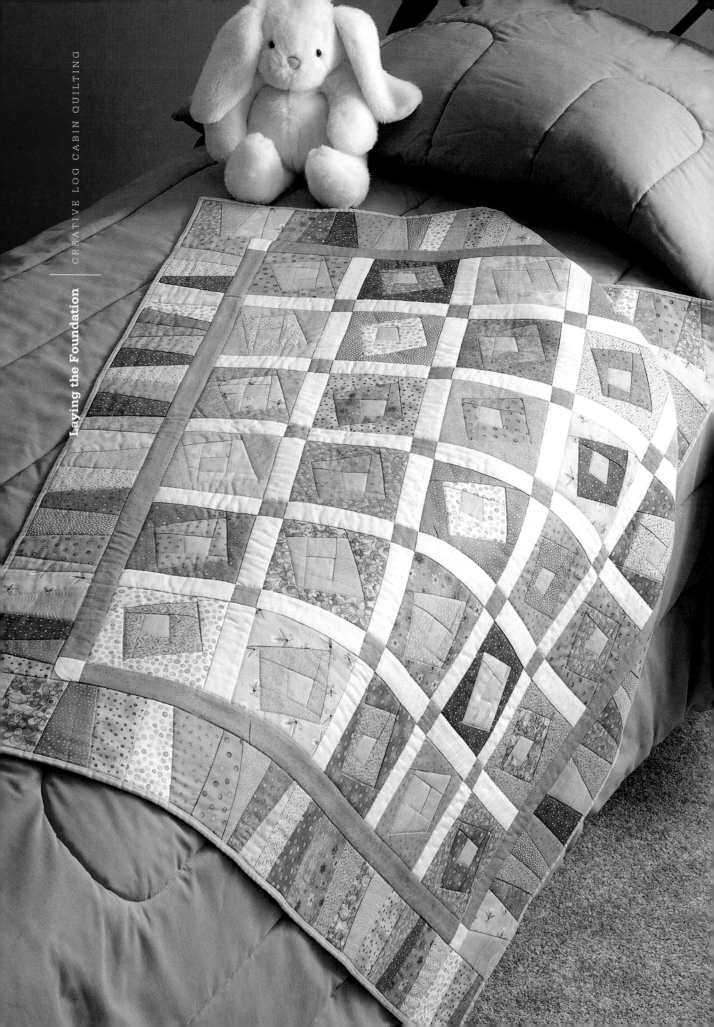

Step 7. Continue to add pieces 3, 4 and 5 in the same manner using the same 2"-wide strip as shown in **Figure 2**.

Step 8. Select a 2¾" x 18" strip of another bright print for pieces 6–9. Sew strips to completed unit as in Steps 5–7 to complete one block. Repeat for 30 blocks. Trim blocks even with foundation patterns.

Completing the Top

Step 1. Cut three strips white-on-white print 5½" by fabric width; subcut strips into 1¾" A sashing strips. You will need 49 A strips.

Step 2. Cut one strip aqua mottled 1¾" by fabric width; subcut strip into 1¾"-square segments for B. You will need 20 B squares.

Step 3. Join five Crazy Log blocks with four A strips to make a block row referring to **Figure 3**; press seams toward A. Repeat for six rows.

Step 4. Join five A strips with four B squares to make a sashing row as shown in **Figure 4**; press seams toward A. Repeat for five rows.

Step 5. Join the block rows with the sashing rows to complete the pieced center; press seams toward sashing rows.

Step 6. Cut four 1¾" x 1¾" C squares white-on-white print. Cut two 1¾" x 30½" D strips and two 1¾" x 36¾" E strips aqua mottled.

Step 7. Sew a D strip to the top and bottom of the pieced center; press seams toward D. Sew C to each end of each E strip; press seams toward E. Sew a C-E strip to opposite long sides of the pieced center; press seams toward strips.

Step 8. Prepare 20 copies of the border paper-piecing pattern. Using the leftover bright print strips, cover paper sections as for making blocks. **Note**: *It may be necessary to cut more strips.*

Step 9. Join five pieced sections to complete a side border strip; repeat for two side strips. Sew a strip to opposite sides of the pieced center; press seams toward the E strips. Trim strips even with quilt center. Repeat with five sections on the top and bottom.

Step 10. Remove all paper foundations.

Finishing the Quilt

Step 1. Prepare quilt top for quilting and quilt.

Step 2. When quilting is complete, trim batting and backing edges even with quilted top.

Step 3. Prepare 5¼ yards yellow stripe binding and bind edges of quilt to finish. 🏠

FIGURE 2 Add pieces 3, 4 and 5.

FIGURE 3 Join 5 Crazy Log blocks with 4 A strips to make a block row.

FIGURE 4 Join 5 A strips with 4 B squares to make a sashing row.

CRAZY LOGS KID'S QUILT Placement Diagram 40½" x 46¾"

Laying the Foundation

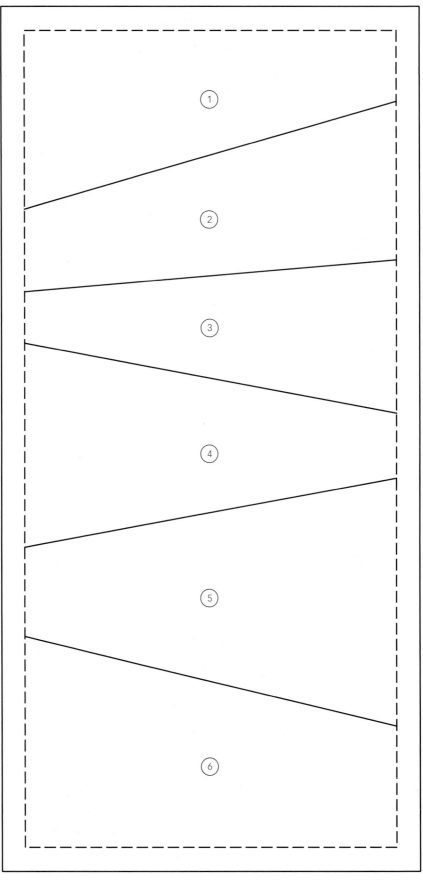

BORDER PAPER-PIECING PATTERN

Make 20 copies

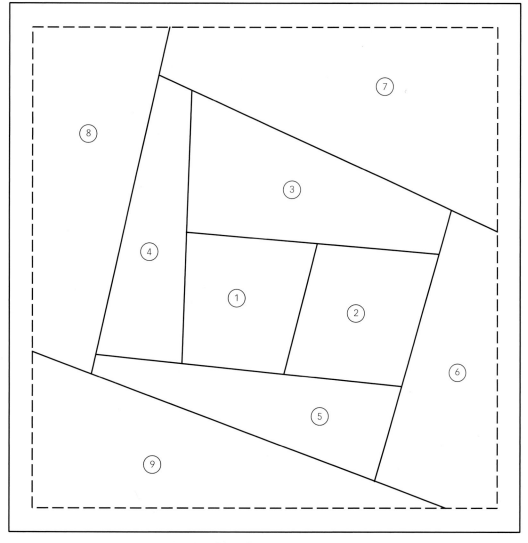

CRAZY LOG PAPER-PIECING PATTERN

Make 30 copies

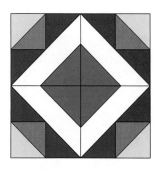

DIAMOND SQUARES
10" x 10" Block

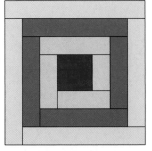

LOG CABIN
10" x 10" Block

Diamonds &
Squares

Log Cabin blocks combine with a paper-pieced block to create a diamond-and-square design.

PROJECT SPECIFICATIONS

Skill Level: Beginner
Quilt Size: 86" x 96"
Block Size: 10" x 10" Block
Number of Blocks: 56

MATERIALS

- ¾ yard pink tone-on-tone
- 1¼ yards each burgundy and green tone-on-tones
- 1½ yards white-on-white print
- 1¾ yards dark blue mottled
- 2 yards light blue tone-on-tone
- Backing 92" x 102"
- Batting 92" x 102"
- Neutral color all-purpose thread
- Quilting thread
- Basic sewing tools and supplies

INSTRUCTIONS

Making Log Cabin Blocks

Step 1. Cut two 3" by fabric width strips burgundy tone-on-tone; subcut strips into 3" square segments for piece 1. Repeat for 28 piece 1 squares.

Step 2. Cut 1¾" by fabric width strips of each of the following fabrics: 13 strips pink tone-on-tone for pieces 2–5; 20 strips dark blue mottled for pieces 6–9; and 27 strips light blue tone-on-tone for pieces 10–13.

Step 3. Place a piece 1 square right sides together with a piece 2 strip and stitch as shown in **Figure 1**; continue adding squares to the strips until all squares have been stitched.

Step 4. Trim the strip even with the squares as shown in **Figure 2**; press seam toward strip to make a 1-2 unit, again referring to **Figure 2**.

Step 5. Continue adding the pieced units to the strips referring to **Figure 3** for order of

FIGURE 1 Place a piece 1 square right sides together with a piece 2 strip and stitch.

FIGURE 2 Trim the strip even with the squares; press seam toward strip.

piecing and color order. Pieces 2, 3, 4 and 5 are pink tone-on-tone; pieces 6, 7, 8 and 9 are dark blue mottled; and pieces 10, 11, 12 and 13 are light blue tone-on-tone.

Step 6. Repeat for 28 Log Cabin blocks; check size and trim to 10½" x 10½". Set aside.

Making Diamond Squares Blocks

Step 1. Make 112 copies of the unit pa-per-piecing pattern.

Step 2. Cut five 3½" by fabric width strips each light blue (1) and green tone-on-tones (2) and 10 strips burgundy tone-on-tone (3 and 4); subcut all strips into 3½" square segments. You will need 56 squares each for pieces 1, 2, 3 and 4.

Step 3. Cut 23 strips white-on-white print 2" by fabric width; subcut strips into 8½" segments; you will need 112 segments for piece 5.

Step 4. Cut six 4" by fabric width strips dark blue mottled; subcut strips into 4" square segments. You will need 56 squares for piece 6.

Step 5. Cut all square pieces on one diagonal to make triangles.

Step 6. Beginning with piece 1 and referring to foundation piecing on page 6–8 and **Figure 3**, add pieces in numerical order to complete units. You will need 112 units.

Step 7. Join four units as shown in **Figure 4** to complete one Diamond Squares block; press seams in one direction. Repeat for 28 blocks.

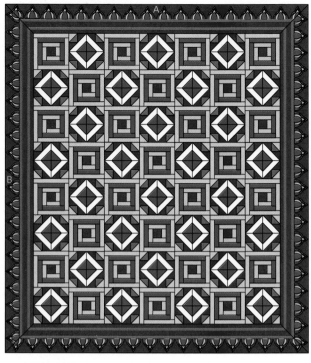

DIAMONDS & SQUARES Placement Diagram 86" x 96"

Completing the Top

Step 1. Join four Log Cabin blocks with three Diamond Squares blocks to make a row as shown in **Figure 5**; press seams toward Log Cabin blocks. Repeat for four rows.

Step 2. Join four Diamond Squares blocks with three Log Cabin blocks to make a row as shown in **Figure 6**; press seams toward Log Cabin blocks. Repeat for four rows.

Step 3. Join the rows referring to the Placement Diagram for positioning of blocks;

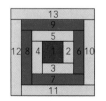

FIGURE 3 Add pieces in numerical order to complete units.

FIGURE 4 Join 4 units to complete 1 Diamond Squares blocks.

FIGURE 5 Join 4 Log Cabin blocks with 3 Diamond Squares blocks to make a row.

FIGURE 6 Join 4 Diamond Squares blocks with 3 Log Cabin blocks to make a row.

press seams in one direction.

Step 4. Cut two 8½" x 88" A strips and two 8½" x 98" B strips from identical sections along the length of the stripe fabric, keeping the same design in the center of each strip. **Note**: *Strips are a little longer than needed to allow for trimming after mitering corners.* Center and sew the B strips to opposite sides and the A strips to the top and bottom of the pieced center, mitering corners. Trim excess seam on the backside and press.

Step 5. Remove paper foundations.

Finishing the Quilt

Step 1. Prepare quilt top for quilting and quilt.

Step 2. When quilting is complete, trim batting and backing edges even with quilted top.

Step 3. Prepare 11 yards green tone-on-tone binding and bind edges of quilt to finish.

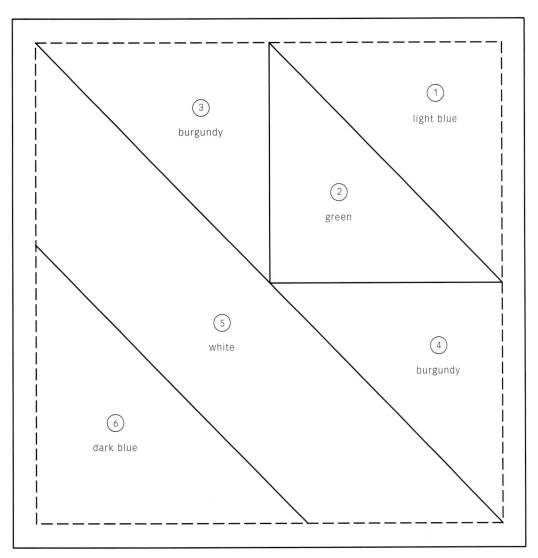

Unit Paper-Piecing Pattern
Make 112 copies

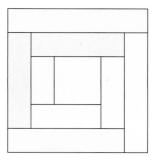

CREAM LOG CABIN
2¼" x 2¼" Block

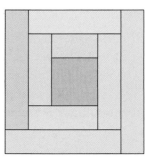

PINK LOG CABIN
2¼" x 2¼" Block

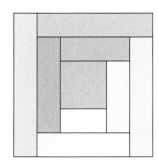

COMBINATION LOG CABIN
2¼" x 2¼" Block

Sweetheart Log Cabin

Tiny Log Cabin blocks pieced in three color configurations create a heart design when stitched together.

PROJECT SPECIFICATIONS

Skill Level: Intermediate
Quilt Size: 22½" x 21¼"
Block Size: 2¼" x 2¼"
Number of Blocks: 30

MATERIALS

- 10–12 light blue scraps
- 10–12 light pink scraps
- 18–20 cream scraps
- ⅛ yard salmon tone-on-tone
- ¼ yard light blue print
- ¼ yard blue/cream stripe for binding
- Backing 29" x 28"
- Lightweight batting 29" x 28"
- Neutral color all-purpose thread
- Contrasting quilting thread
- Basic sewing tools and supplies

INSTRUCTIONS

Step 1. Make copies of block piecing units referring to patterns for number of each to copy.
Step 2. Complete foundation piecing on paper copies referring to the instructions on page 6–8.

Step 3. When all blocks have been pieced, trim even with outside edges of paper at outer seam line.
Step 4. Arrange blocks in five rows of six blocks each referring to **Figure 1** for placement. Join blocks in rows; press seam allowances of adjoining rows in opposite directions. Join rows to complete the pieced center.

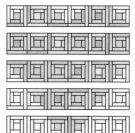

FIGURE 1 Arrange blocks in 5 rows of 6 blocks each.

Step 5. Cut two 2½" x 14" A and two 2" x 15¾" B strips from cream scraps. Sew an A strip to the top and bottom, and B strips to opposite sides of the pieced center; press seams toward strips. Remove paper foundations from blocks.
Step 6. Cut two 1" x 17" C strips and two 1" x 16¾" D strips salmon tone-on-tone. Sew

C strips to the top and bottom, and D strips to opposite sides of the pieced center; press seams toward strips.

Step 7. Cut two 3" x 18" E strips and two 3" x 16¾" F strips light blue print. Cut four 3" x 3" G squares pink scrap. Sew E strips to the top and bottom of the pieced center; press seams toward strips. Sew G to each end of each F strip and sew to the remaining sides to complete the top; press seams toward strips.

Finishing the Quilt

Step 1. Prepare quilt top for quilting and quilt. **Note:** *The sample was hand-quilted in the ditch of border seams and using the patterns provided with the heart shape in the center and the remaining center background area in a 1½" cross-hatch grid using contrasting quilting thread.*

Step 2. When quilting is complete, trim batting and backing edges even with quilted top.

Step 3. Prepare 2¾ yards blue/cream stripe binding and bind edges of quilt to finish. 🏠

Laying the Foundation

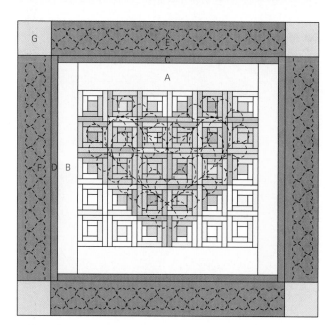

SWEETHEART LOG CABIN Placement Diagram 22½" x 21¼"

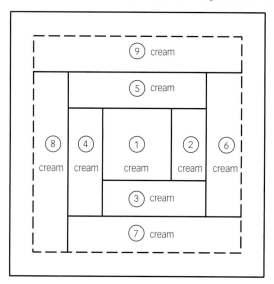

CREAM LOG CABIN PATTERN

Make 6 copies

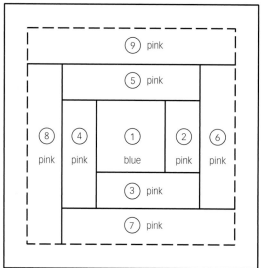

PINK LOG CABIN PATTERN

Make 14 copies

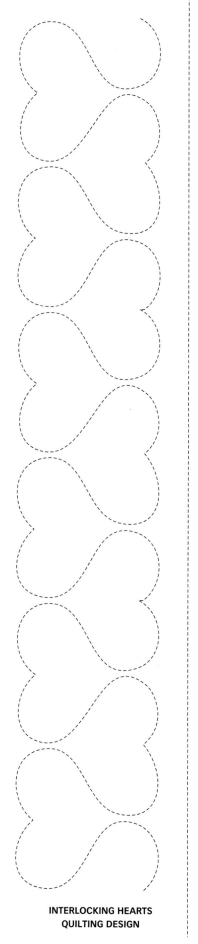

Place line at border seam

**INTERLOCKING HEARTS
QUILTING DESIGN**

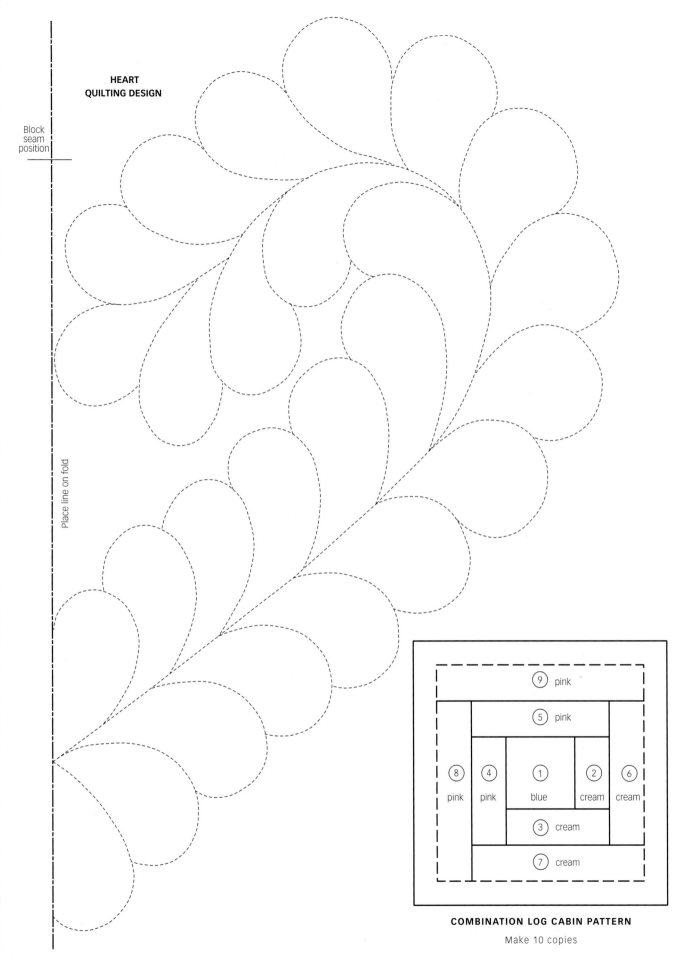

**HEART
QUILTING DESIGN**

Block
seam
position

Place line on fold

COMBINATION LOG CABIN PATTERN

Make 10 copies

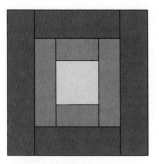

COURTHOUSE STEPS
7" x 7" Block

Hanging
Diamonds

The Courthouse Steps block takes on a new look when placed on the diagonal and separated by sashing to make rows.

PROJECT SPECIFICATIONS

Skill Level: Beginner
Quilt Size: 45½" x 51½"
Block Size: 7" x 7"
Number of Blocks: 16

MATERIALS

- ⅝ yard tan mottled
- ¾ yard burgundy mottled
- 1 yard medium brown mottled
- 1 yard dark brown print
- 1⅛ yards dark green tone-on-tone
- Backing 52" x 58"
- Batting 52" x 58"
- Neutral color all-purpose thread
- Quilting thread
- Basic sewing tools and supplies

INSTRUCTIONS
Making Blocks

Step 1. Prepare 16 copies of the Hanging Diamonds paper-piecing pattern.
Step 2. Cut sixteen 2⅝" x 2⅝" squares tan mottled for block centers.
Step 3. Cut seven 1¾" by fabric width strips medium brown mottled and twelve 2" by fabric width strips burgundy mottled.
Step 4. Pin a tan mottled square to the unmarked side of one paper-piecing pattern in the No. 1 position; pin a medium brown mottled strip to the square with right sides together on the No. 2 edge of the square as shown in **Figure 1**.
Step 5. Turn paper over; stitch on the line between pieces 1 and 2; turn pattern over. Press piece 2 to the right side; trim excess even with piece 1. Repeat on the No. 3 side of the center square with the same medium brown mottled strip.

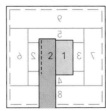

FIGURE 1 Stitch a medium brown mottled strip to the square with right sides together on the No. 2 edge of the square.

Step 6. Continue to add strips to the paper-piecing pattern referring to pattern for color and order of stitching until all strips have been added. Trim edges even with paper pattern. Repeat for 16 blocks.

Making Side and Corner Triangles

Step 1. Make 24 copies of the B side border triangle paper-piecing pattern.

Step 2. Cut twelve 3¾" x 3¾" squares tan mottled; cut each square in half on one diagonal to make triangles for piece 1.

Step 3. Cut five strips medium brown mottled and 13 strips dark brown print 2¼" by fabric width for pieces 2 and 3.

Step 4. Pin a piece 1 triangle to each paper pattern and add strips 2 and 3 as in Steps 4–6 for Making Blocks. Repeat for 24 units.

Step 5. Make 16 copies of the C corner border triangle paper-piecing pattern.

Step 6. Cut eight 3" x 3" squares medium brown mottled; cut each square on one diagonal to make the No. 1 triangles.

Step 7. Using leftover dark brown mottled strips from B side border triangles, complete 16 C corner border triangles as in Steps 4–6 for Making Blocks.

Completing the Top

Step 1. Sew a C triangle to two adjacent sides of a completed block as shown in **Figure 2**; press seams away from C. Repeat for eight units.

Step 2. Sew a B triangle to one side of the

HANGING DIAMONDS Placement Diagram 45½" x 51½"

pieced unit as shown in **Figure 3**; press seams away from B. Repeat for eight units.

Step 3. Sew B to two opposite sides of a pieced block as shown in **Figure 4**; press seams away from B. Repeat for eight units.

Step 4. Join the pieced units as shown in Figure 5 to complete one row; press seams in one direction. Repeat for four rows.

Step 5. Cut three 2½" x 40" strips dark green tone-on-tone for D.

Step 6. Join the block rows with the D strips; press seams toward D.

Step 7. Cut (and piece) two 3½" x 40" E strips and two 3½" x 52" F strips dark green tone-

FIGURE 2 Sew a C triangle to 2 adjacent sides of a completed block.

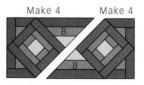

FIGURE 3 Sew a B triangle to 1 side of the pieced unit.

FIGURE 4 Sew B to 2 opposite sides of a pieced block.

FIGURE 5 Join the pieced units to complete 1 row.

on-tone. Sew E to the top and bottom, and F to opposite long sides of the pieced center; press seams toward strips. Remove all paper foundations.

Step 2. When quilting is complete, trim batting and backing edges even with quilted top.

Step 3. Prepare 6 yards dark green tone-on-tone binding and bind edges of quilt to finish. 🏠

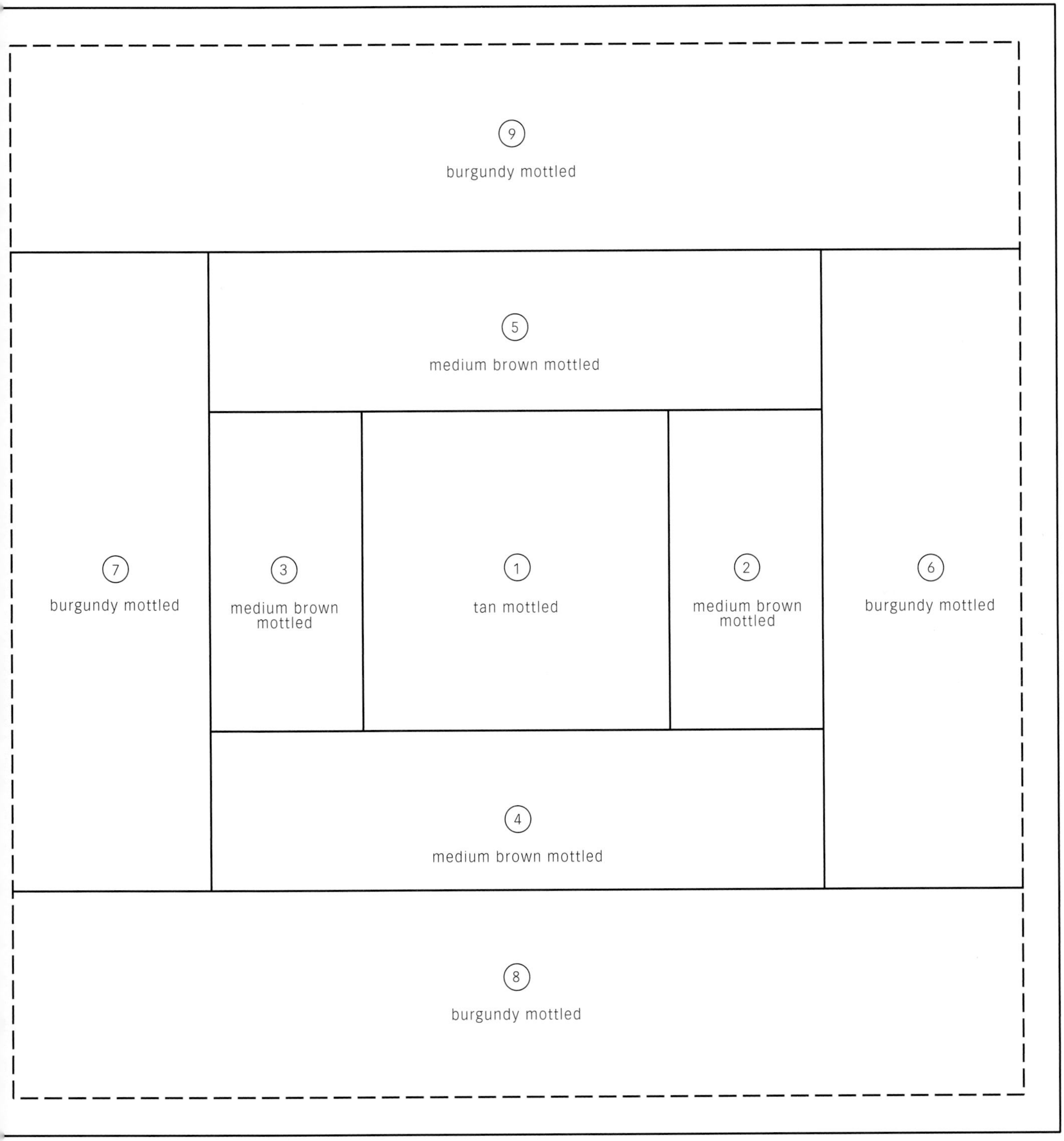

Finishing the Quilt

Step 1. Prepare quilt top for quilting and quilt.

⑨
burgundy mottled

⑤
medium brown mottled

⑦
burgundy mottled

③
medium brown
mottled

①
tan mottled

②
medium brown
mottled

⑥
burgundy mottled

④
medium brown mottled

⑧
burgundy mottled

HANGING DIAMONDS PAPER-PIECING PATTERN

Make 16 copies

B SIDE BORDER TRIANGLE PAPER-PIECING PATTERN

Make 24 copies

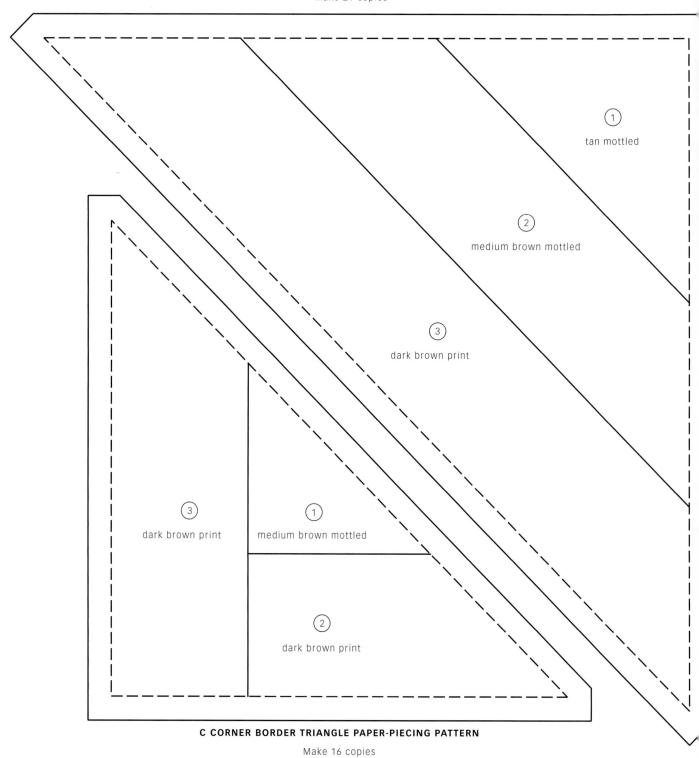

1
tan mottled

2
medium brown mottled

3
dark brown print

3
dark brown print

1
medium brown mottled

2
dark brown print

C CORNER BORDER TRIANGLE PAPER-PIECING PATTERN

Make 16 copies

Plaid Lap Robe & Candle Mat

Use paper foundations to piece accurate triangle-shaped Log Cabin blocks with woven plaids in a variety of colors.

Plaid Lap Robe

PROJECT SPECIFICATIONS

Skill Level: Intermediate

Quilt Size: 42" x 48"

MATERIALS

- ⅛ yard tan solid
- ¼ yard each 12 light plaids
- ¼ yard each 12 dark plaids
- ½ yard black solid
- Backing 48" x 56"
- Fusible batting 48" x 56"
- Neutral color all-purpose thread
- Quilting thread
- Basic sewing tools and supplies

INSTRUCTIONS

Making Pieced Units

Step 1. Cut all plaid fabrics into 1½" by fabric width strips.

Step 2. Cut two 1½" by fabric width strips tan solid; subcut into fifty-one 1½" squares for piece 1. Repeat with black solid to make 43 squares for piece 1. Set aside three each tan and black squares for candle mat.

Step 3. Make 88 copies of the A unit pattern and eight copies each of the B and B unit reversed patterns.

Step 4. Pin a piece 1 tan solid square to the unmarked side of the A unit paper pattern to cover the piece 1 area on the marked side; pin a light plaid piece 2 to piece 1 referring to foundation piecing on page 49.

Step 5. Stitch strips in numerical order to the paper pattern to complete 48 light plaid A units referring to **Figure 1**. Repeat with black solid No. 1 pieces to complete 40 dark plaid A units as shown in **Figure 2**. **Note:** *Vary the fabric strips used in piece 4, as these pieces*

FIGURE 1 Complete light plaid A units as shown.

FIGURE 2 Complete dark plaid A units as shown.

Laying the Foundation

will be touching each other in the finished top.

Step 6. Repeat to complete eight each dark plaid B and BR units referring to **Figure 3**.

Completing the Top

Step 1. Join five dark and six light plaid A units to make a row as shown in **Figure 4**; repeat for eight rows; press seams toward darker units.

Step 2. Sew B and BR to the end of each row, again referring to **Figure 4**; press seams toward B and BR.

Step 3. Join the rows referring to the Placement Diagram for positioning; press seams in one direction.

Finishing the Quilt

Step 1. Prepare quilt top for quilting using fusible batting referring to manufacturer's instructions and quilt.

Step 2. When quilting is complete, trim batting and backing edges even with quilted top.

Step 3. Prepare 5½ yards black solid binding and bind edges of quilt.

Candle Mat

PROJECT SPECIFICATIONS

Mat Size: 14" x 12"

MATERIALS

- Leftover fabric scraps from lap robe
- Fusible batting 16" x 14"
- Backing 16" x 14"
- Neutral color all-purpose thread
- Quilting thread
- Basic sewing tools and supplies

INSTRUCTIONS

Step 1. Make six copies of the A unit pattern.

Step 2. Complete six A units as for lap robe.

Step 3. Join one dark plaid and two light plaid A units as shown in **Figure 5**; repeat with one light plaid and two dark plaid A units, again referring to **Figure 5**. Press seams toward darker A units. Join the pieced units to complete the candle mat top.

Step 4. Finish as for lap robe, preparing 1½ yards black solid binding to finish. ✿

PLAID CANDLE MAT

Placement Diagram 14" x 12"

Easy Binding Technique for Hexagon Shapes

Sew binding to one side of the hexagon mat, stopping at the point where the two triangle units meet as shown in **Figure 6**.

Remove mat from under sewing-machine foot; fold binding up along the seam line between the two triangle units as shown in **Figure 7**.

Fold binding down along the next edge of mat as shown in **Figure 8**; sew along the edge to next point. Continue sewing, folding the binding at each turn.

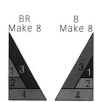

FIGURE 3 Complete dark plaid B and BR units as shown.

FIGURE 4 Join 5 dark and 6 light plaid A units to make a row; add B and BR.

FIGURE 5 Join A units as shown.

FIGURE 6 Stop stitching at the point where 2 triangle units meet.

FIGURE 7 Fold binding back along the seam line between the 2 triangle units.

FIGURE 8 Fold binding back and sew to next point.

Laying the Foundation

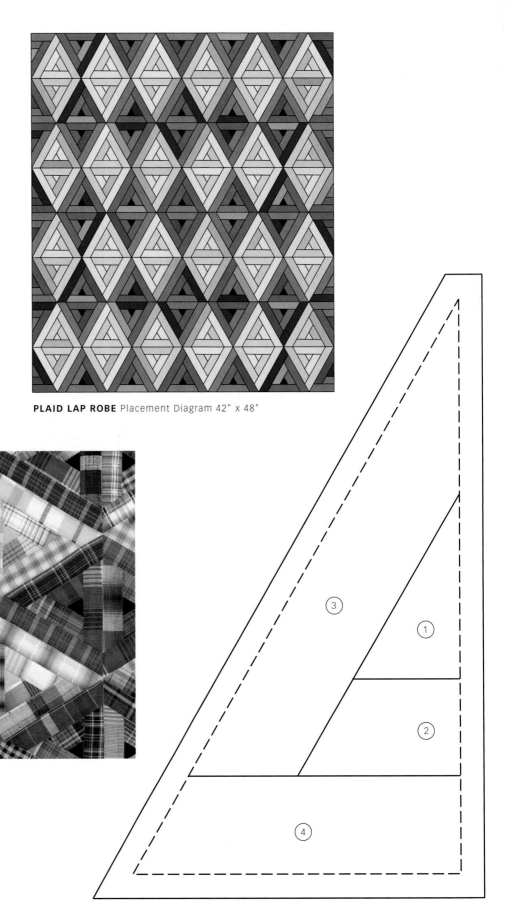

PLAID LAP ROBE Placement Diagram 42" x 48"

③

①

②

④

B UNIT REVERSED

Make 8 copies

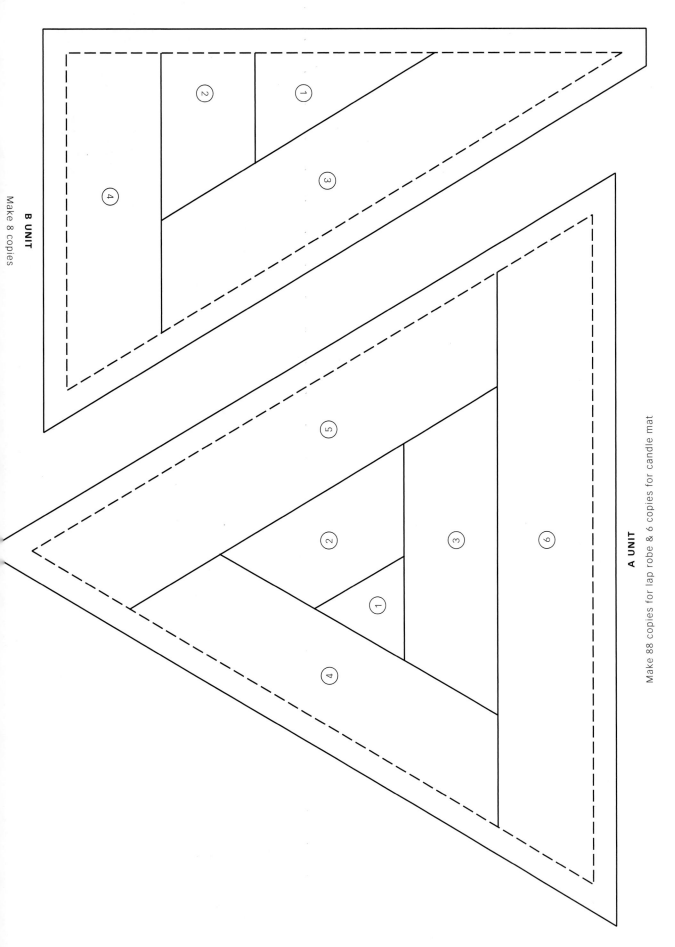

B UNIT
Make 8 copies

A UNIT
Make 88 copies for lap robe & 6 copies for candle mat

49

CABINS OF THE BEAR
14" x 14" Block

Cabins of the Bear

Log Cabin blocks bordered by Bear Paw units create the larger blocks in this diagonal-set bed quilt.

PROJECT SPECIFICATIONS

Skill Level: Intermediate
Quilt Size: 88¾" x 111⅜"
Block Size: 14" x 14"
Number of Blocks: 18

MATERIALS

- 1⅜ yards muslin for foundation piecing
- 1⅝ yards green tone-on-tone for first border and binding
- 1½ yards total assorted prints for Log Cabin centers
- 2¼ yards green print for blocks and sashing squares·
- 3¼ yards cream tone-on-tone for background and sashing
- 4¼ yards large green floral for setting triangles and borders
- Backing 95" x 118"
- Batting 95" x 118"
- Neutral color all-purpose thread
- Quilting thread
- Basic sewing tools and supplies

INSTRUCTIONS

Making Blocks

Step 1. Cut eighteen 9½" x 9½" squares muslin.

Step 2. Cut eighteen 2" x 2" squares green print for block centers.

Step 3. From the assorted prints, cut a total of 30 strips 1¼" by fabric width. **Note:** *This cut assumes all fabric widths are 40" minimum. More or fewer strips may be needed during Log Cabin assembly.*

Step 4. To make one Log Cabin block center, place a 2" square right side up in the center of a muslin foundation square. Select one of the assorted prints and cut a strip 2" long.

Step 5. With right sides together and matching raw edges, place a strip on the left side of the 2" square; sew and press open. Referring to the full-size piecing diagram given on page 54, cut remaining logs the sizes shown from the remaining prints. Complete 18 Log Cabin block centers referring to pages 9–11 for instructions. **Note:** *Color placement for logs varies from block to block to give the block centers a scrappy look.*

Step 6. When sewing is complete, trim the pieced Log Cabin block centers to 6½" x 6½".

Step 7. Cut fourteen 2½" by fabric width strips cream tone-on-tone; subcut five of these strips into seventy-two 2½" square segments for A. Subcut the remaining nine strips into seventy-two 4½" B rectangles.

Step 8. Cut eleven 2⅞" by fabric width strips each cream tone-on-tone and green print; subcut strips into 2⅞" square segments for C. You will need 144 C squares of each fabric.

Step 9. Cut fourteen 2½" by fabric width strips green print; subcut five of these strips into seventy-two 2½" square segments for D. Subcut the remaining nine strips into seventy-two 4½" E rectangles.

Step 10. Layer a cream tone-on-tone C square with a green print C square with right sides together. Draw a diagonal line from corner to corner on the wrong side of the lighter color square.

Step 11. Sew ¼" on each side of the drawn line as shown in **Figure 1**; cut apart on the drawn line to reveal two C units as shown in **Figure 2**. Repeat for all C triangles.

Step 12. To piece one Cabins of the Bear block, sew a C unit to D as shown in **Figure 3**; repeat for two C-D and two C-D reversed units, again referring to **Figure 3**.

Step 13. Sew a C-D and C-DR unit to opposite sides of B as shown in **Figure 4**; repeat for two B-C-D units.

Step 14. Sew a B-C-D unit to opposite sides of a Log Cabin center as shown in **Figure 5**. Press seams away from the center.

Step 15. Sew a C unit to E; repeat for two C-E and two C-E reversed units as shown in **Figure 6**.

Step 16. Join two C units with A; repeat for two C-A and C-A reversed units as shown in **Figure 7**.

Step 17. Join a C-E unit with a C-A unit; repeat for reversed units as shown in **Figure 8**. Repeat for two each C-A-E and C-A-E reversed units.

Step 18. Join the pieced units with B and stitch to remaining sides of the Log Cabin center as shown in **Figure 9** to complete one block; repeat for 18 blocks.

Completing the Top

Step 1. Cut three 14½" by fabric width strips cream tone-on-tone; subcut strips into forty-eight 2½" F sashing strips.

Step 2. Cut two 2½" by fabric width strips green print; subcut strips into thirty-one 2½" G sashing squares.

Step 3. Cut three 23⅞" x 23⅞" squares large green floral; cut each square in half on both diagonals to make H triangles as shown in **Figure 10**.

FIGURE 1 Sew ¼" on each side of the drawn line.

FIGURE 2 Cut apart on the drawn line to reveal 2 C units.

FIGURE 3 Sew a C unit to D; repeat for reversed unit.

FIGURE 4 Sew C-D and C-DR to B.

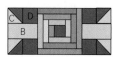

FIGURE 5 Sew B-C-D to opposite sides of a Log Cabin center.

FIGURE 6 Sew a C unit to E; repeat for a reversed unit.

FIGURE 7 Join 2 C units with A; repeat for reversed units.

FIGURE 8 Join a C-E unit with a C-A unit; repeat for reversed units.

Step 4. Cut two 13⅝" x 13⅝" squares large green floral; cut each square in half on one diagonal to make I triangles, again referring to **Figure 10**.

Step 5. Arrange the pieced blocks in diagonal rows with the F and G sashing pieces, and the H and I triangles referring to **Figure 11**, joining blocks in rows with F pieces and joining G pieces with H to make sashing rows.

Step 6. Press seams away from blocks and away from F strips; press seams toward H and I triangles. **Note:** *If all stitching is perfectly accurate, the top should now measure 71¼" x 93⅞".*

Step 7. Cut and piece two 2" x 74¼" J strips and two 2" x 93⅞" K strips green tone-on-tone. Sew K strips to opposite long sides, and J strips to the top and bottom of the pieced center; press seams toward strips.

Step 8. Cut and piece two 8" x 89¼" L strips and two 8" x 96⅞" M strips large green floral. Sew M strips to opposite long sides, and L strips to the top and bottom of the pieced center; press seams toward strips.

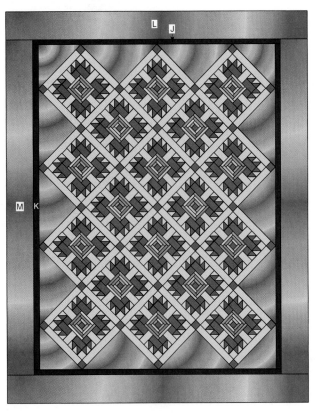

CABINS OF THE BEAR Placement Diagram 88¾" x 111⅜"

Finishing the Quilt

Step 1. Prepare quilt top for quilting and quilt.

Step 2. When quilting is complete, trim batting and backing edges even with quilted top.

Step 3. Prepare 11⅝ yards green tone-on-tone binding and bind edges of quilt to finish. 🏠

FIGURE 10 Cut squares as shown to make H and I triangles.

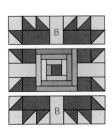

FIGURE 9 Join the pieced units to complete 1 block.

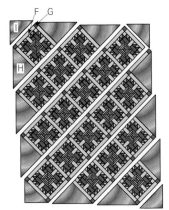

FIGURE 11 Arrange the pieced blocks in diagonal rows with the F and G sashing pieces and the H and I triangles.

Laying the Foundation

13
1¼" x 6½"

9
1¼" x 5"

5
1¼" x 3½"

10   6   2   1   4   8   12
1¼" x 5"   1¼" x 3½"   1¼" x 2"   2" x 2"   1¼" x 2¾"   1¼" x 4¼"   1¼" x 5¾"

3
1¼" x 2¾"

7
1¼" x 4¼"

11
1¼" x 5¾"

LOG CABIN BLOCK CENTER

Full-size piecing diagram

CAROLINA CABINS
10" x 10" Block

Carolina
Cabins

The traditional Carolina Lily is given a new twist with Log Cabin flower heads.

PROJECT SPECIFICATIONS
Skill Level: Intermediate
Quilt Size: 42" x 42
Block Size: 10" x 10"
Number of Blocks: 4

MATERIALS
- Scrap lightest pink for piece 1
- ⅛ yard light pink for pieces 2 and 3
- ⅛ yard medium pink for piece 4 and 5
- ⅓ yard green tone-on-tone No. 1 for stems, leaves, piece 8 and sashing squares
- ½ yard dark pink for piece 4 and borders
- ½ yard muslin for foundations
- ⅔ yard green tone-on-tone No. 2 for borders and binding
- ⅔ yard cream-on-cream print for background and sashing
- 1 yard check print for borders
- Backing 48" x 48"
- Batting 48" x 48"
- Neutral color and green all-purpose thread
- Quilting thread
- ⅔ yard fusible web
- Basic sewing tools and supplies

INSTRUCTIONS
Cutting
Step 1. Cut two 6½" by fabric width strips muslin; subcut strips into twelve 6½" square segments for foundations.

Step 2. Cut twelve 1½" x 1½" squares lightest pink for piece 1.

Step 3. Cut two 1½" by fabric width strips light pink; subcut into twelve 1½" squares and twelve 2½" rectangles for pieces 2 and 3.

Step 4. Cut two 1½" by fabric width strips medium pink; subcut strips into twelve 2½" and twelve 3½" rectangles for pieces 4 and 5.

Step 5. Cut three 1½" by fabric width strips dark pink; subcut strips into twelve 3½" and twelve 4½" rectangles for pieces 6 and 7.

Step 6. Cut one 2½" by fabric width strip green tone-on-tone 1; subcut strip into twelve 2½" square segments for piece 8. Draw a diagonal line from corner to corner on the wrong side of each square.

Step 7. Cut four 6½" x 6½" squares cream-on-cream print for A.

Step 8. Cut eight 2½" x 4½" rectangles cream tone-on-tone for B.

Step 9. Cut nine 2½" x 2½" squares green tone-on-tone No. 1 for C sashing squares.

Step 10. Cut one 10½" by fabric width strip cream-on-cream print; subcut into twelve 2½" segments for D sashing strips.

Step 11. Cut two 1" x 26½" E strips and two 1" x 27½" F strips green tone-on-tone 2.

Step 12. Cut two 1" x 27½" G strips and two 1" x 28½" H strips dark pink.

Step 13. Cut two 6½" x 28½" I strips and two 6½" x 40½" J strips check print.

Step 14. Cut two 1" x 40½" K strips and two 1" x 41½" L strips dark pink.

Step 15. Cut two 1" x 41½" M strips and two 1" x 42½" N strips green tone-on-tone 2.

Completing the Blocks

Step 1. To piece one Log Cabin unit, place one piece 1 right side up and in approximately 1" on one corner of a muslin foundation square as shown in **Figure 1**. With right sides together and raw edges even, place the piece 2 square on top of the piece 1 square. Sew a ¼" seam on the right side, open and press.

Step 2. Referring to the Log Cabin Unit piecing diagram, continue sewing the pieces in the same manner in numerical order through piece 7.

Step 3. Place a piece 8 square on the corner of the pieced section referring to the Log Cabin Unit piecing diagram; stitch on the marked line and trim excess green fabric to ¼" as shown in **Figure 2**. Press the triangle down to complete one Log Cabin unit.

Step 4. When the unit is finished, trim to measure 4½" x 4½"; repeat for 12 Log Cabin units.

Step 5. Iron fusible web to the wrong side of the remaining green tone-on-tone No. 1. Prepare templates for the appliquéd stems and leaves using the full-size patterns given.

Step 6. Trace appliqué shapes on the paper side of the fused fabric as directed on patterns for number to cut; cut out shapes on traced lines. Remove paper backing.

Step 7. Fuse stems and leaves to the A squares referring to the block drawing for placement of pieces. **Note:** *The stem piece extends into the seam allowance at all ends.*

Step 8. Using thread to match the fabric, stitch all around each shape using a machine buttonhole stitch.

Step 9. Join two Log Cabin units with B as shown in **Figure 3**; press seams toward B.

Step 10. Sew B to a Log Cabin unit and join with an appliquéd A square as shown in **Figure 4**; press seams toward B and A.

Step 11. Join the pieced units to complete one block as shown in **Figure 5**; repeat for four blocks.

Completing the Quilt Top

Step 1. Join two blocks with three D strips to make a block row referring to **Figure 6**; repeat for two rows. Press seams toward D.

Step 2. Join three C squares with two D strips to make a sashing row as shown in **Figure 7**;

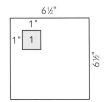

FIGURE 1 Place piece 1 right side up on 1 corner of a foundation square 1" from edges of square.

FIGURE 2 Trim excess green piece to ¼".

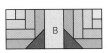

FIGURE 3 Join 2 Log Cabin units with B.

FIGURE 4 Sew B to a Log Cabin unit and join with an appliquéd A square.

FIGURE 5 Join the pieced units to complete 1 block.

FIGURE 6 Join 2 blocks with 3 D strips to make a block row.

FIGURE 7 Join 3 C squares with 2 D strips to make a sashing row.

Laying the Foundation

repeat for three sashing rows. Press seams toward D.

Step 3. Join the block rows with the sashing rows referring to the Placement Diagram; press seams toward sashing rows.

Step 4. Sew E strips to opposite sides, and F strips to the top and bottom of the pieced center; press seams toward strips.

Step 5. Sew G strips to opposite sides, and H strips to the top and bottom of the pieced center; press seams toward strips.

Step 6. Sew I strips to opposite sides, and J strips to the top and bottom of the pieced center; press seams toward strips.

Step 7. Sew K strips to opposite sides, and L strips to the top and bottom of the pieced center; press seams toward strips.

Step 8. Sew M strips to opposite sides, and N strips to the top and bottom of the pieced center; press seams toward strips.

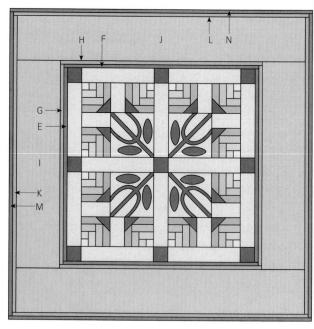

CAROLINA CABINS Placement Diagram 42" x 42"

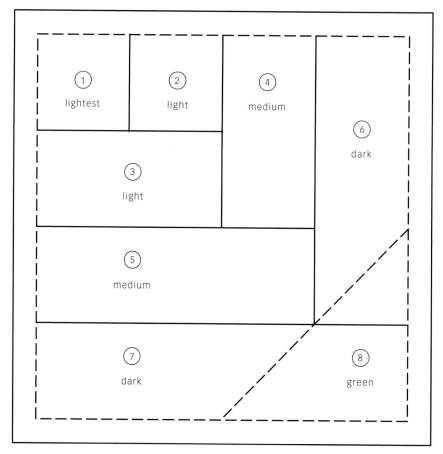

LOG CABIN UNIT

Full-size piecing diagram

Finishing the Quilt

Step 1. Prepare quilt top for quilting and quilt.

Step 2. When quilting is complete, trim batting and backing edges even with quilted top.

Step 3. Prepare 5 yards green tone-on-tone No. 2 binding and bind edges of quilt to finish. 🏠

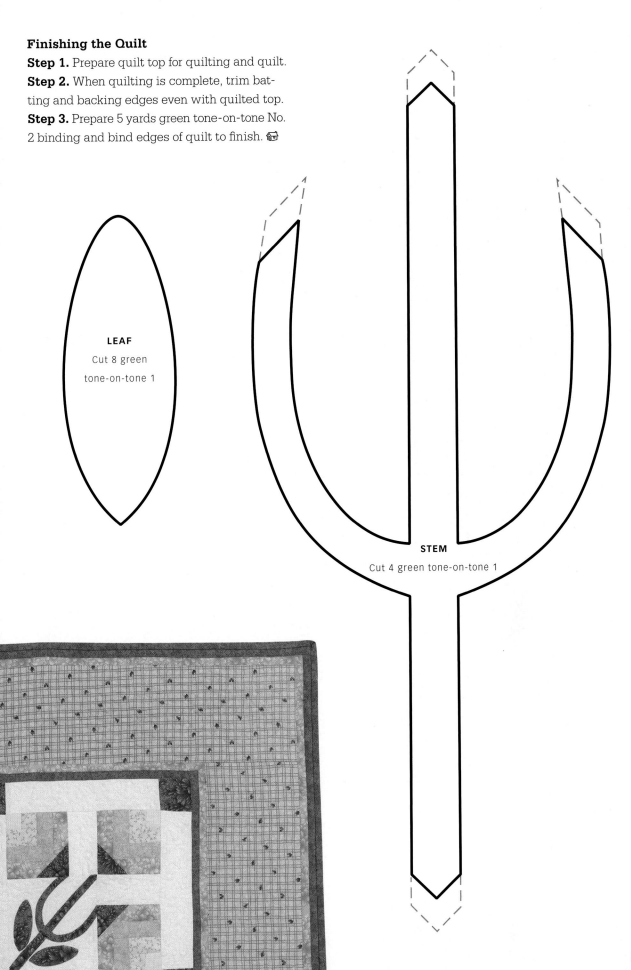

LEAF
Cut 8 green
tone-on-tone 1

STEM
Cut 4 green tone-on-tone 1

The "logs" of Log Cabin quilts can be any size and a variety of shapes. Put together they build beautiful quilts that will last a lifetime.

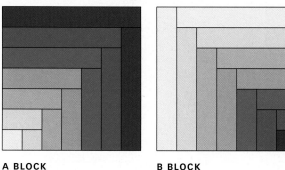

A BLOCK
14" x 14" Block

B BLOCK
14" x 14" Block

DESIGN > LUCY A. FAZELY &
MICHAEL L. BURNS

Bear Paw Star

Strips are added to only one side of the center in the one-sided Log Cabin blocks used in this quilt.

PROJECT NOTE

Seven different blue fabrics were used in the Log Cabin blocks in this quilt. They are all either mottled or tone-on-tones. It is difficult to give each fabric a name, so we have assigned each fabric a number. The lowest number represents the lightest fabric, and the highest number represents the darkest fabric. The numbers in between are for fabrics ranging from light to dark. It is important to assign a number to the fabrics and remember the designation when cutting and piecing blocks.

PROJECT SPECIFICATIONS

Skill Level: Intermediate
Quilt Size: 96" x 96"
Block Size: 7" x 7" and 14" x 14"
Number of Blocks: 80 small, 16 large

MATERIALS

- 1 yard each fabrics 1–6
- 2⅞ yards white-with-blue print
- 3⅜ yards dark navy mottled 7
- Backing 102" x 102"
- Batting 102" x 102"

- Neutral color all-purpose thread
- Quilting thread
- Basic sewing tools and supplies

C BLOCK
7" x 7" Block

C BLOCK REVERSED
7" x 7" Block

D BLOCK
7" x 7" Block

D BLOCK REVERSED
7" x 7" Block

E BLOCK
7" x 7" Block

INSTRUCTIONS

Completing the Blocks

Step 1. Cut and piece two 6½" x 84½" Y strips and two 6½" x 96½" Z strips dark navy mottled 7; set aside for borders.

Step 2. Cut 10 dark navy mottled 7 strips 2¼" by fabric width for binding; set aside.

Step 3. Cut seven strips each 2½" by fabric width from blue fabrics 1–7.

Step 4. Cut nine strips each blue fabrics 1 and 7, eight strips each blue fabrics 2, 3, 4, 5 and 6, and 64 strips white-with blue print 1½" by fabric width.

Step 5. Join one 2½"-wide blue 1 strip and one 2½"-wide blue 2 strip with right sides together along length; press seams toward darkest fabric. Subcut strip set into eight 2½" segments for A referring to **Figure 1**.

Step 6. Join one 2½"-wide blue 6 strip with one 2½"-wide blue 7 strip with right sides together along length; press seams toward darkest fabric. Subcut strip set into eight 2½" segments for B referring to **Figure 2**.

Step 7. Join one 1½"-wide blue 1 strip with one 1½"-wide white-with-blue print strip with right sides together along length; repeat for two strip sets. Press seams toward darkest fabric. Subcut strip set into thirty-two 1½" segments for C referring to **Figure 3**.

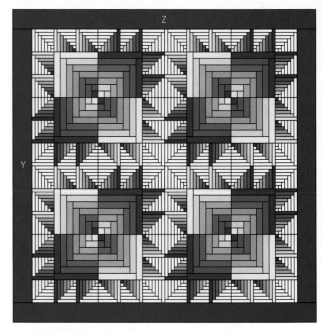

Bear Paw Star Placement Diagram 96" x 96"

Step 8. Join one 1½"-wide blue 7 strip with one 1½"-wide white-with-blue print strip with right sides together along length; repeat for two strip sets. Press seams toward darkest fabric. Subcut strip set into thirty-two 1½" segments for D referring to **Figure 4**.

Step 9. Join two 1½"-wide white-with-blue print strips with right sides together along length; press. Subcut strip set into sixteen 1½" segments for E referring to **Figure 5**.

Step 10. Beginning with A units, stitch units to a blue 2 strip, press and trim referring

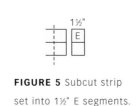

FIGURE 5 Subcut strip set into 1½" E segments.

FIGURE 6 Stitch an A unit to a blue 2 strip; press and trim as shown.

FIGURE 1 Subcut strip set into 2½" A segments.

FIGURE 3 Subcut strip set into 1½" C segments.

FIGURE 2 Subcut strip set into 2½" B segments.

FIGURE 4 Subcut strip set into 1½" D segments.

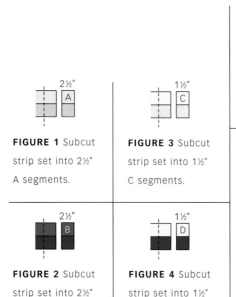

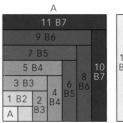

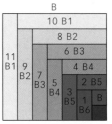

FIGURE 7 Continue to add strips to the same 2 sides of the pieced unit to complete A blocks. Repeat for B blocks.

to instructions on page 9–11 and **Figure 6**. Continue to add strips to the same two sides of the pieced unit to complete one A block as shown in **Figure 7**; repeat for eight A blocks. Repeat with B units to complete eight B blocks.

Step 11. Repeat with C, D and E units to complete C, D and E blocks referring to **Figure 8** for color.

Completing the Top

Step 1. Join an A block with two each C and CR blocks, and one E block to make an A block unit as shown in **Figure 9**; repeat for eight A block units. Press seams toward A blocks.

Step 2. Join a B block with two each D and DR blocks, and one E block to make a B block unit as shown in **Figure 10**; repeat for eight B block units. Press seams toward B blocks.

Step 3. Join two each A and B block units

to complete an A/B block unit as shown in **Figure 11**; repeat for four units. Press seams in one direction.

Step 4. Join the four A/B block units to complete the pieced center referring to the Placement Diagram for positioning. Press seams in one direction.

Step 5. Using the previously cut Y and Z strips, sew Y strips to opposite sides and Z strips to the top and bottom of the pieced center; press seams toward strips.

Finishing the Quilt

Step 1. Prepare quilt top for quilting and quilt.

Step 2. When quilting is complete, trim batting and backing edges even with the quilted top.

Step 3. Prepare 11 yards of binding from the previously cut 2¼"-wide dark blue mottled strips and bind edges of quilt to finish. 🏠

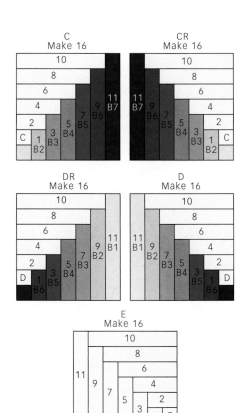

FIGURE 8 Complete blocks as shown making half-white/half-blue C, CR, D and DR blocks and all-white E blocks.

FIGURE 9 Join an A block with 2 each C and CR blocks and 1 E block to make an A block unit.

FIGURE 10 Join a B block with 2 each D and DR blocks and 1 E block to make a B block unit.

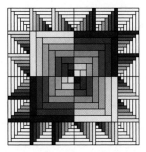

FIGURE 11 Join 2 each A and B block units to complete an A/B block unit.

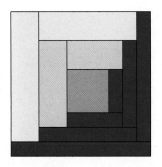

LOG CABIN
4⅜" x 4⅜" Block

Red
Starburst

Diamond units with narrow strips can be accurately pieced using foundation-piecing methods.

PROJECT SPECIFICATIONS

Skill Level: Advanced
Quilt Size: 43" x 43"
Block Size: 4⅜" x 4⅜ "
Number of Blocks: 8

MATERIALS

- ⅓ yard dark pink mottled
- ½ yard medium pink tone-on-tone
- ⅝ yard light pink mottled
- ⅝ yard white-on-white print
- 2 yards burgundy mottled
- Backing 49" x 49"
- Batting 49" x 49"
- Neutral color all-purpose thread
- Quilting thread
- Basic sewing tools and supplies

INSTRUCTIONS

Making A and B Units

Step 1. Make 16 copies each of A and B foundations using patterns given on page 70.

Step 2. To make A and B foundations, cut 19 strips burgundy mottled 1" by fabric width for the dark sides of the units.

Step 3. Cut eight light pink mottled and six medium pink tone-on-tone 1¼" by fabric width strips for light sides of the A and B units.

Step 4. Cut two strips dark pink mottled 1½" by fabric width for piece 1 centers of the A and B units.

Step 5. Referring to **Figure 1**, complete 16 each A and B units using foundation papers and previously cut strips, and referring to patterns for order of piecing and page 6–8 for instructions.

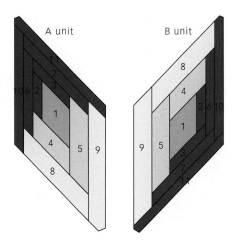

FIGURE 1 Make A and B units as shown.

Making Log Cabin Blocks

Step 1. Make eight copies of Log Cabin block foundations using pattern given.

Step 2. Cut five strips burgundy mottled 1" by fabric width for dark side of block.

Step 3. Cut eight 1⅞" x 1⅞" squares dark pink mottled for center piece 1.

Step 4. Cut two strips each medium pink tone-on-tone and light pink mottled 1½" by fabric width.

Step 5. Referring to **Figure 2**, complete eight Log Cabin blocks using foundation papers and previously cut strips and referring to patterns for order of piecing and page 6–8 for instructions.

Making Corner Units

Step 1. Make four copies of the corner unit foundation using pattern given.

Step 2. Cut one 6¼" x 6¼" square light pink mottled; cut the square on both diagonals to make piece 1 triangles.

Step 3. Cut two strips each dark pink mottled, medium pink tone-on-tone and burgundy mottled 1½" by fabric width.

Step 4. Referring to **Figure 3**, complete four corner units using foundation papers and previously cut strips and referring to patterns for order of piecing and page 6–8 for instructions.

Completing the Top

Step 1. Cut four 7½" x 7½" C squares white-on-white print. Cut each square on both

RED STARBURST Placement Diagram 43" x 43"

diagonals to make C triangles as shown in **Figure 4**.

Step 2. Join one corner unit with two each A and B units, one Log Cabin block and two C triangles to make a corner section as shown in **Figure 5**.

Step 3. Join two each A and B units, and one Log Cabin block to make a side section as shown in **Figure 6**.

Step 4. Join two side sections, one corner section and two C triangles as shown in **Figure 7**; repeat for two units.

Step 5. Join one corner section with one side/corner section and one C triangle as shown in **Figure 8**; repeat for two units.

FIGURE 2 Complete Log Cabin blocks as shown.

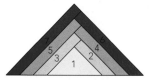

FIGURE 3 Complete corner units as shown.

FIGURE 4 Cut squares on both diagonals to make C triangles.

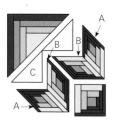

FIGURE 5 Join 1 corner unit with 2 each A and B units, 1 Log Cabin block and 2 C triangles to make a corner section.

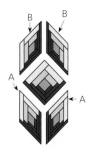

FIGURE 6 Join 2 each A and B units and 1 Log Cabin block to make a side section.

Step 6. Join the two units with two C triangles as shown in **Figure 9** to complete the pieced center.

Step 7. Cut two 2" x 30½" D strips and two 2" x 33½" E strips burgundy mottled. Sew D strips to the top and bottom, and E strips to opposite sides of the pieced center; press seams toward strips.

Step 8. Cut two 2" x 33½" F strips and two 2" x 36½" G strips white-on-white print. Sew the F strips to the top and bottom and the G strips to opposite sides of the pieced center; press seams toward strips.

Step 9. Cut two 4" x 36½" H strips and two 4" x 43½" I strips burgundy mottled. Sew the H strips to opposite sides and I to the top and bottom of the pieced center; press seams toward strips.

Finishing the Quilt

Step 1. Prepare quilt top for quilting and quilt.

Step 2. When quilting is complete, trim batting and backing edges even with the quilted top.

Step 3. Prepare 5 yards burgundy mottled binding and bind edges to finish. 🏠

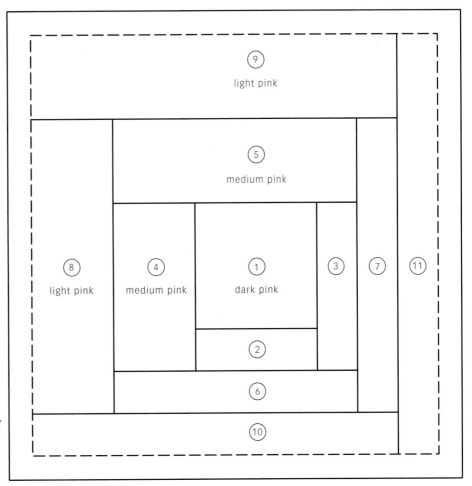

LOG CABIN BLOCK
Make 8 copies
Use burgundy mottled for unmarked logs

FIGURE 7 Join 2 side sections, 1 corner section and 2 C triangles.

FIGURE 8 Join 1 corner section with 1 side/corner section and 1 C triangle.

FIGURE 9 Join the 2 units with 2 C triangles.

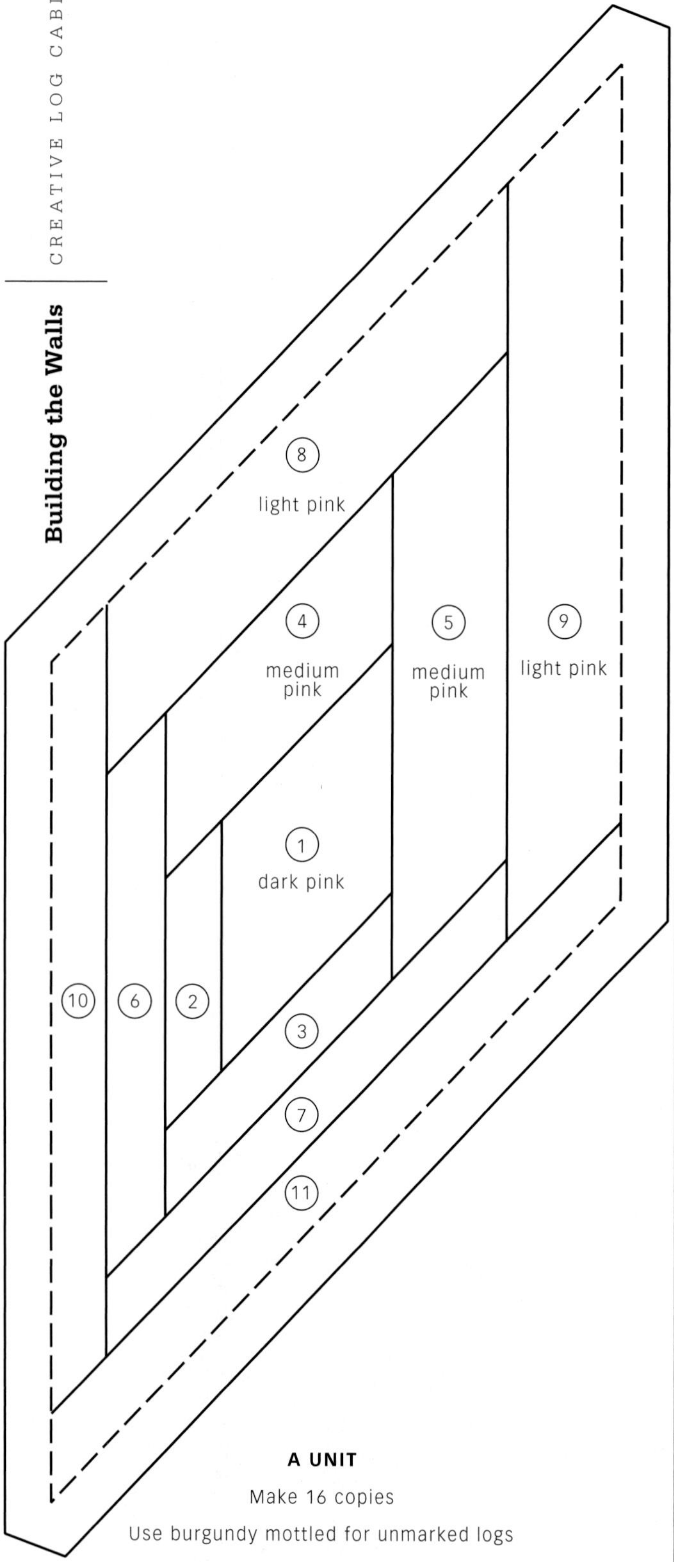

Building the Walls

A UNIT

Make 16 copies

Use burgundy mottled for unmarked logs

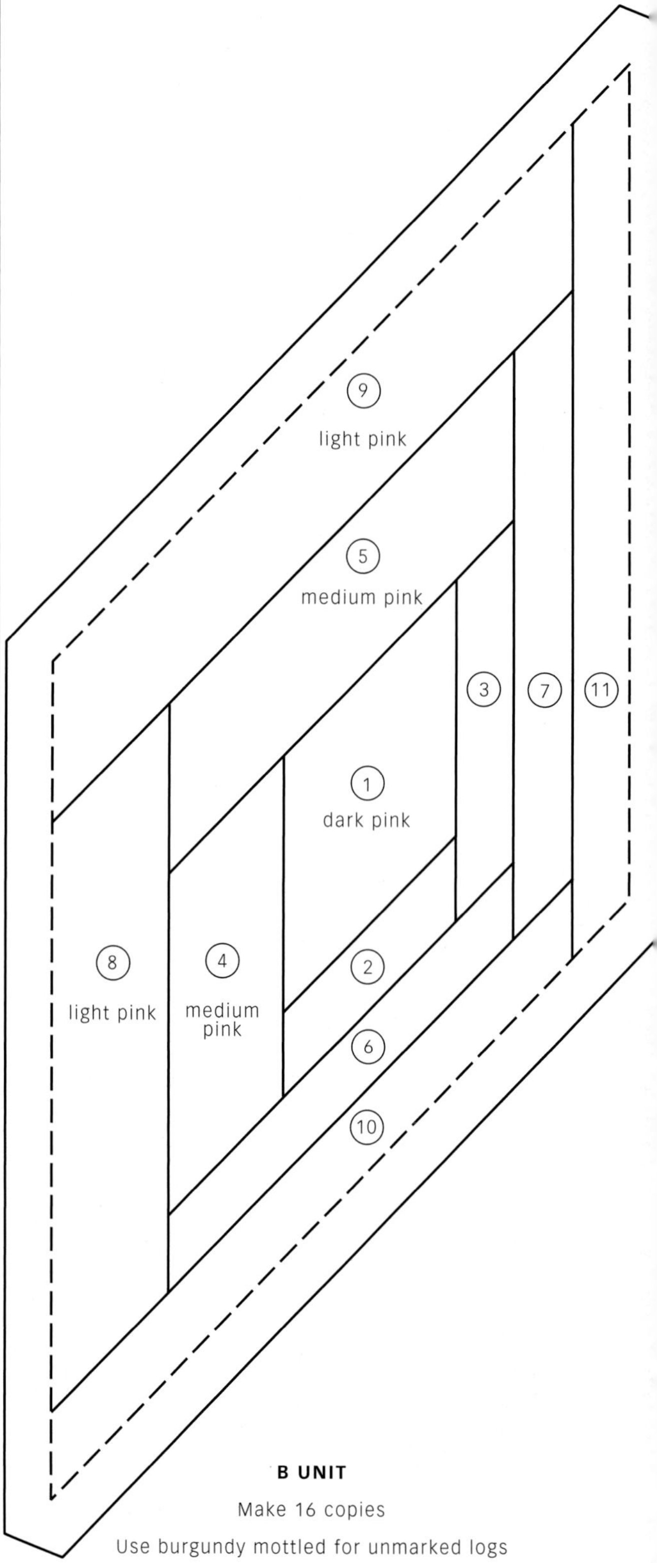

B UNIT

Make 16 copies

Use burgundy mottled for unmarked logs

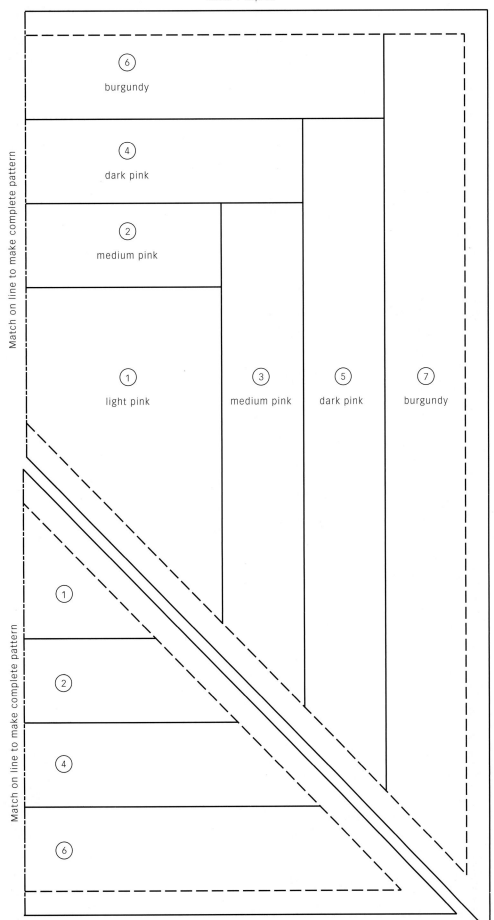

CORNER UNIT

Make 4 copies

Match on line to make complete pattern

⑥ burgundy

④ dark pink

② medium pink

① light pink

③ medium pink

⑤ dark pink

⑦ burgundy

Match on line to make complete pattern

① ② ④ ⑥

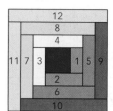

LOPSIDED LOG CABIN

11¼" x 11¼" Block

Lopsided
Log Cabin

Bright-color yellow fabrics help spread the illusion of sunshine and happiness in this bed-size quilt.

PROJECT SPECIFICATIONS

Skill Level: Beginner
Quilt Size: 68" x 88"
Block Size: 11¼" x 11¼"
Number of Blocks: 30

MATERIALS

- ½ yard each 7 different orange and yellow fabrics (prints, mottled, tone-on-tones)
- ¼ yard burgundy solid
- ⅝ yard orange print for binding
- 1 yard yellow mottled
- 1⅓ yards yellow print
- Backing 74" x 94"
- Batting 74" x 94"
- Neutral color all-purpose thread
- Quilting thread
- Basic sewing tools and supplies

INSTRUCTIONS

Making Log Cabin Center Blocks

Step 1. Cut two 2½" by fabric width strips burgundy solid.

Step 2. Cut the seven different yellow and orange fabrics into 1½" by fabric width strips.

Step 3. Assign numbers 1–7 to each yellow and orange fabric to determine the rounds.

Step 4. Sew orange fabric 1 to a burgundy solid strip with right sides together along length; press seams toward darkest fabric. Repeat for two strip sets.

Step 5. Subcut strip sets into 2½" segments as shown in **Figure 1**. You will need 30 segments.

Step 6. Sew strips to the pieced segments with yellow fabrics on one side and orange on the other and in numerical order as shown in **Figure 2** and referring to page 9–11 for instructions. Complete 30 Log Cabin units. Measure and trim to 8½" x 8½".

2½"

FIGURE 1

Subcut strip set into 2½" segments.

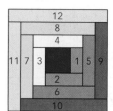

FIGURE 2 Sew strips to center in numerical order, placing yellow and orange strips as shown.

Building the Walls

Completing Blocks

Step 1. Make 120 copies of the corner unit pattern for foundations.

Step 2. Referring to **Figure 3** and using the remaining 1½" by fabric width strips yellow and orange fabrics, prepare 60 each yellow and orange foundation-pieced triangles referring to pattern and page 6–8 for instructions.

Step 3. Trim corner triangles on outside solid lines.

Step 4. Sew an orange triangle to each orange side of a Log Cabin unit and a yellow triangle to the remaining sides to complete one block referring to **Figure 4**; press seams toward corner triangles. Repeat for 30 blocks.

Completing the Top

Step 1. Cut four 17¼" x 17¼" squares yellow print for A; cut each square on both diagonals to make A triangles. You will need 16 A triangles.

Step 2. Cut one 8⅞" x 8⅞" square yellow print for B; cut the square on one diagonal to make two B triangles.

Step 3. Cut and piece two 6½" x 88½" strips yellow mottled for C.

Step 4. Arrange the completed blocks with A triangles in diagonal rows referring to **Figure 5**. Join in rows; press seams in one direction. Join rows and add B to opposite corners to complete the pieced center; press seams in one direction.

Step 5. Sew a C strip to opposite long sides to

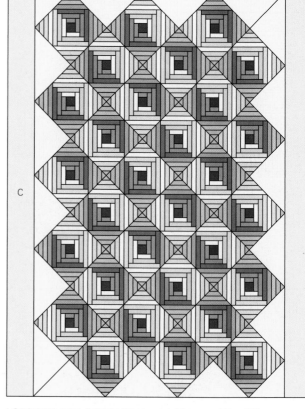

LOPSIDED LOG CABIN Placement Diagram 68" x 88"

complete the pieced top; press seams toward C.

Finishing the Quilt

Step 1. Prepare quilt top for quilting and quilt.

Step 2. When quilting is complete, trim batting and backing edges even with the quilted top.

Step 3. Prepare 9 yards orange print binding and bind edges to finish. ⌂

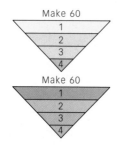

FIGURE 3 Complete corner units in numerical order to make 60 each orange and yellow units.

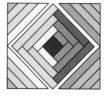

FIGURE 4 Sew corner units to a Log Cabin unit.

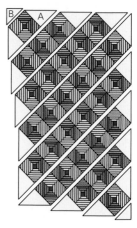

FIGURE 5 Arrange blocks with A in diagonal rows; add B to opposite corners.

CORNER UNIT FOUNDATION

Make 120 copies

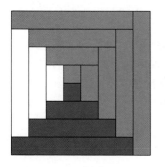

OVERLAPPING LOGS 1

10" x 10" Block

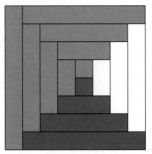

OVERLAPPING LOGS 2

10" x 10" Block

Overlapping Cabins

No two blocks are the same in this complicated Log Cabin pattern.

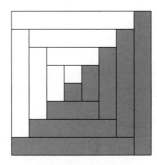

CORNER BLOCK 1

10" x 10" Block

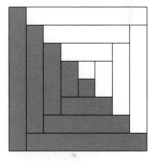

CORNER BLOCK 2

10" x 10" Block

PROJECT SPECIFICATIONS

Skill Level: Advanced

Quilt Size: 91" x 99¾"

Block Size: 10" x 10"

Number of Blocks: 72

MATERIALS

- 1 fat quarter each 7 different purple fabrics
- 1 fat quarter each 7 different blue fabrics
- 1 fat quarter each 7 different pink fabrics
- 1 fat quarter each 7 different green fabrics
- ½ yard each blue, purple, pink and green fabrics
- ¾ yard green marbled for binding
- 3¼ yards white floral for background
- Backing 97" x 106"
- Batting 97" x 106"
- All-purpose thread to match fabrics
- Quilting thread
- Basic sewing tools and supplies

INSTRUCTIONS

Step 1. Cut all colored fabrics into 1¾" by fabric width strips. **Note:** *For fat quarters, cut strips across the 22" width.*

Step 2. Cut and piece two 3½" x 80½" A strips and two 3½" x 96½" strips white floral. Set aside for borders.

Step 3. Cut remainder of white floral into 1¾" by fabric width strips.

Step 4. Cut one strip white floral into 1¾" squares for piece 1.

Step 5. Choose one colored strip; cut a 1¾" square from the strip. Sew the colored square to a white floral square for block center as shown in **Figure 1**; press seams toward colored square.

FIGURE 1 Sew the colored square to a white floral square for block center.

Step 6. Sew the same-colored strip to one side and a white floral strip to the opposite side of the pieced unit as shown in **Figure 2**; press seams toward strips and trim even to complete a unit.

Step 7. Continue adding strips in numerical order in this manner to complete one Corner Block 1 referring to **Figure 3** for piecing order and to page 9–11 for instructions.

Step 8. Repeat to complete two each Corner Blocks 1 and 2, and seven each Overlapping Logs 1 and 2 in each color family referring to **Figure 3** for order of piecing and to **Figure 4** for positioning of colored fabrics and white floral for all blocks in one color family. **Note:** *Each vertical row consists of one each Corner Block 1 (CB1) and 2 (CB2) and seven Overlapping Logs 1 (OL1) or 2 (OL2). Two vertical rows make the complete section of one color family. The rows are pieced in the same way*

from one color family to another. Substitute the pink, blue or green fabrics for the purple fabrics shown in the **Figure 4** *example to complete the rows for each color family.*

Step 9. Repeat for 72 blocks. Measure and trim blocks to 10½" x 10½".

Completing the Top

Step 1. Arrange the pieced blocks in eight vertical rows of nine blocks keeping same color family in rows, again referring to **Figure 4**. Join blocks in rows; press seams in one direction. Join rows referring to the Placement Diagram for positioning of colors; press seams in one direction.

Step 2. Sew an A strip to the top and bottom and B strips to opposite sides of the pieced center; press seams toward strips.

Step 3. Join leftover strips on short ends to make four 1¾" x 96½" C strips and three 1¾" x

91½" D strips referring to **Figure 5**.

Step 3. Join two C strips with right sides together along length; press seams in one direction. Repeat for two strips. Sew a strip to opposite long sides of the pieced center; press seams toward strips. Repeat with two D strips on the bottom and one on the top of the pieced center; press seams toward strips.

Finishing the Quilt

Step 1. Prepare quilt top for quilting and quilt.

Step 2. When quilting is complete, trim batting and backing edges even with quilt top all around.

Step 3. Prepare 11 yards green marbled binding and bind edges of quilt to finish. 🏠

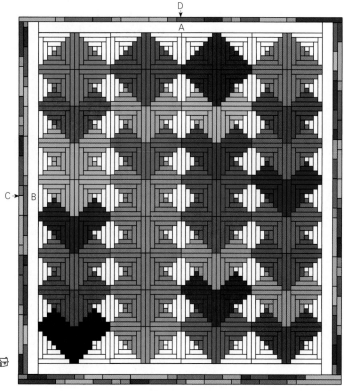

OVERLAPPING LOG CABINS Placement Diagram 91" x 99¾"

FIGURE 2 Sew the same-colored strip to 1 side and a white floral strip to the opposite side of the pieced unit.

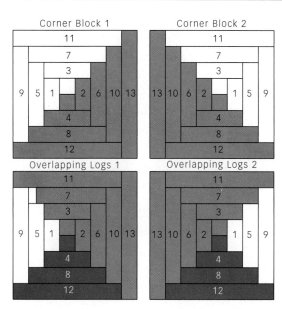

Corner Block 1

Corner Block 2

Overlapping Logs 1

Overlapping Logs 2

FIGURE 3 Add strips in numerical order to complete blocks.

FIGURE 5 Join the leftover strips on short ends to make border strips.

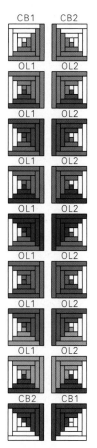

CB1 CB2
OL1 OL2
OL1 OL2
OL1 OL2
OL1 OL2
OL1 OL2
OL1 OL2
OL1 OL2
CB2 CB1

FIGURE 4 Complete blocks placing colored fabrics in the positions shown.

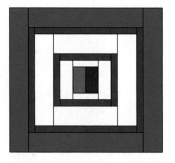

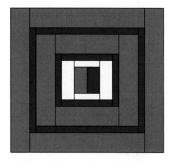

DESIGN > CONNIE RAND

BLUE COURTHOUSE STEPS VARIATION
10" x 9¾" Block

RED COURTHOUSE STEPS VARIATION
10" x 9¾" Block

Courthouse Steps
Variation

Red, white and blue fabrics make a patriotic statement in the Courthouse Steps Variation quilt.

PROJECT SPECIFICATIONS
Skill Level: Beginner
Quilt Size: 62" x 90"
Block Size: 10" x 9¾"
Number of Blocks: 40

MATERIALS
- 1 yard blue solid
- 1⅛ yards white-on-white print
- 1⅝ yards red solid
- 1⅞ yards red star print
- 2 yards blue star print
- Backing 68" x 96"
- Batting 68" x 96"
- Neutral color all-purpose thread
- Quilting thread
- Basic sewing tools and supplies

INSTRUCTIONS
Making Blocks
Step 1. Cut three strips each red and blue star prints 1¼" by fabric width. Join one red and one blue strip with right sides together along length; press seam toward blue star print. Repeat for three strip sets.
Step 2. Subcut strip sets into forty 2¼" A

segments as shown in **Figure 1**.
Step 3. Cut four 1" by fabric width strips for B and seven 1¼" by fabric width strips for C from white-on-white print.
Step 4. Cut 24 strips each red and blue star prints 1" by fabric width for D.
Step 5. Cut 12 white-on-white print, 18 blue solid and 30 red solid 1¾" by fabric width strips for E.
Step 6. Sew A segments to B strips; press seams toward B and trim strips even with A as shown in **Figure 2**. Repeat on opposite side of A, again referring to **Figure 2**.
Step 7. Sew A-B units to C strips as in Step 6 and as shown in **Figure 3**; press seams toward C.

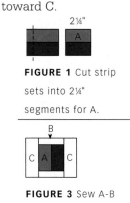

FIGURE 1 Cut strip sets into 2¼" segments for A.

FIGURE 3 Sew A-B units to C strips.

FIGURE 2 Sew A segments to B strips and trim strips even with A; repeat on opposite side of A.

Step 8. To piece one blue block, add red star print D strips to each side of an A-B-C unit as shown in **Figure 4**; press seams toward D.

Step 9. Add white-on-white print E strips, red star print D strips and blue solid E strips in the same manner to complete one Blue Courthouse Steps Variation block, referring to **Figure 5** for order of piecing. Repeat for 20 blocks.

Step 10. Repeat Steps 8 and 9 to complete 20 red blocks using blue star print D strips and red solid E strips as shown in **Figure 6**.

Completing the Top

Step 1. Join three blue blocks with two red blocks to make a row as shown in **Figure 7**; press seams toward red blocks. Repeat for four rows. Join three red blocks with two blue blocks, again referring to **Figure 7**; press seams toward red blocks. Repeat for four rows.

Step 2. Join rows referring to the Placement Diagram for positioning; press seams in one direction.

Step 3. Cut and piece two strips each 2½" x 78½" for F and 2½" x 54½" for G from blue star print. Sew F to opposite long sides and G to the top and bottom of the pieced center; press seams toward strips.

Step 4. Cut and piece two strips each 4½" x 82½" for H and 4½" x 62½" for I from red star print. Sew H to opposite long sides and I to the top and bottom of the pieced center; press seams toward strips.

COURTHOUSE STEPS VARIATION Placement Diagram 62" x 9(

FINISHING THE QUILT

Step 1. Prepare quilt top for quilting and quilt.

Step 2. When quilting is complete, trim batting and backing edges even with quilted top.

Step 3. Prepare 8¾ yards blue star print binding and bind edges of quilt to finish. 🏠

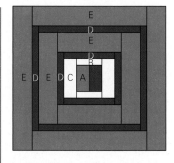

FIGURE 6 Add strips to an A-B-C unit to complete 1 red block.

FIGURE 4 Add red star print D strips to A-B-C units.

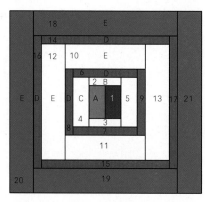

FIGURE 5 Continue adding strips to complete 1 blue block.

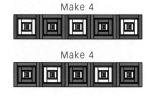

Make 4

Make 4

FIGURE 7 Join blocks in rows.

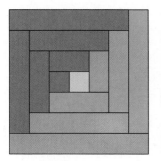

LOG CABIN
10½" x 10½" Block

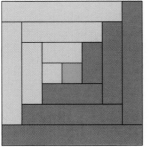

LOG CABIN
10½" x 10½" Block

Batik
Bedspread

Use batik fabrics pieced in five different Log Cabin variations to create a patterned quilt.

PROJECT SPECIFICATIONS

Skill Level: Intermediate
Quilt Size: 84" x 105"
Block Size: 10½" x 10½"
Number of Blocks: 80

MATERIALS

- 1½ yards orange batik
- 2 yards purple batik
- 2⅜ yards lime green batik
- 4¾ yards fern print batik
- Backing 90" x 111"
- Batting 90" x 111"
- Neutral color all-purpose thread
- Quilting thread
- Basic sewing tools and supplies

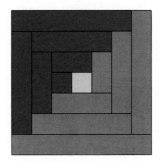

LOG CABIN
10½" x 10½" Block

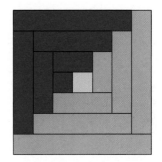

LOG CABIN
10½" x 10½" Block

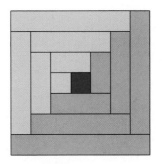

LOG CABIN
10½" x 10½" Block

INSTRUCTIONS

Step 1. Cut 10 strips 2¼" by fabric width fern print batik for binding; set aside. Cut all remaining fabrics into 2" by fabric width strips.

Step 2. Cut forty 2" squares from lime green batik strips.

Step 3. Cut thirty-six 2" squares from orange batik strips.

Step 4. Cut four 2" squares from purple batik strips.

Step 5. Referring to **Figure 1** for color and order of piecing and to the instructions on page 9–11, piece Log Cabin blocks.

Step 6. Lay the blocks out and join in 10 rows of eight blocks each referring to **Figure 2**; press seams in one direction.

Step 7. Join the block rows; press seams in one direction to complete the pieced top.

Finishing the Quilt

Step 1. Prepare quilt top for quilting and quilt.

Step 2. When quilting is complete, trim batting and backing edges even with quilted top.

Step 3. Prepare 10¾ yards fern print batik binding and bind edges of quilt to finish. 🏠

BATIK BEDSPREAD Placement Diagram 84" x 105"

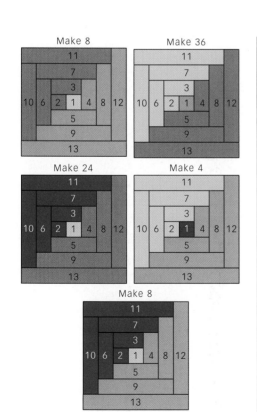

FIGURE 1 Piece Log Cabin blocks in 5 different color combinations as shown.

FIGURE 2 Join the rows to complete the pieced top.

COLOR KEY
- Purple batik
- Orange batik
- Fern print batik
- Lime green batik

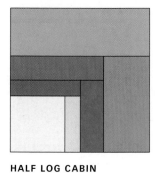

HALF LOG CABIN
9" x 9" Block

Images of Africa

Uneven-width jungle-print strips are added to two adjacent sides of a center square to make half Log Cabin blocks.

PROJECT SPECIFICATIONS

Skill Level: Beginner
Quilt Size: 72" x 90"
Block Size: 9" x 9"
Number of Blocks: 52

MATERIALS

- ½ yard each brown, light brown and tan/sand prints
- ½ yard each 4 different animal prints
- ¾ yard zebra print
- 1 yard dark brown mottled
- 1 yard green mottled
- 1⅛ yards green zebra print
- 1¾ yards brown mottled
- Backing 78" x 96"
- Batting 78" x 96"
- Neutral color all-purpose thread
- Quilting thread
- Basic sewing tools and supplies

INSTRUCTIONS

Making the Blocks

Step 1. Cut two 1½" by fabric width strips each brown mottled, dark brown mottled, each animal print and brown, light brown and tan/ sand prints.

Step 2. Cut seven green zebra print and nine green mottled 2" by fabric width strips.

Step 3. Cut three 3½" by fabric width strips each brown mottled, dark brown mottled, each animal print and brown, light brown and tan/ sand prints.

Step 4. Cut six 4" by fabric width strips zebra print; subcut into 4" square segments for A. You will need 52 A squares.

Step 5. Sew an A square to one 1½"-wide animal print strip; repeat with 13 A squares on each animal print strip. Cut and press units as shown in **Figure 1**.

Step 6. Sew the stitched units to the 1½"-wide strips of each brown as shown in **Figure 2** (there are five browns listed). **Note:** *Try to*

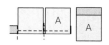

FIGURE 1 Cut and press units.

FIGURE 2 Sew stitched units to the 1½"-wide strips.

evenly distribute these fabrics to add variety to blocks.

Step 7. Repeat with 2"-wide strips and then 3½"-wide strips to complete 52 blocks with varying placement of fabric strips referring to **Figure 3**. **Note:** *Green zebra print 2"-wide strips are used in the No. 3 position and green mottled strips are used in the No. 4 position in every block.* Measure blocks and trim to 9½" x 9½". Set aside four blocks for borders.

Completing the Top

Step 1. Arrange blocks in eight rows of six blocks each referring to the Placement Diagram for positioning of blocks. Join blocks in rows; press seams in one direction. Join rows to complete the pieced center; press seams in one direction.

Step 2. Cut and piece two 1½" x 54½" B strips and two 1½" x 72½" C strips green mottled.

Step 3. Cut and piece two 2½" x 54½" D strips and two 2½" x 72½" E strips dark brown mottled.

Step 4. Cut and piece two 6½" x 54½" F strips and two 6½" x 72½" G strips brown mottled.

Step 5. Sew a B strip to a D strip to an F strip with right sides together along length as shown in **Figure 4**; repeat for two strips. Press seams toward darker fabric strips. Sew a strip to the top and bottom of the pieced center with the B strip on the inside; press seams toward strips.

Step 6. Sew a C strip to an E strip to a G strip with right sides together along length, again referring to **Figure 4**; repeat for two strips. Press seams toward darker fabric strips.

IMAGES OF AFRICA Placement Diagram 72" x 90"

Step 7. Sew a Half Log Cabin block to the end of each strip referring to **Figure 5**; press seams toward strips. Sew a strip to opposite long sides of the pieced center with the C strip on the side to complete the top; press seams toward strips.

Finishing the Quilt

Step 1. Prepare quilt top for quilting and quilt.

Step 2. When quilting is complete, trim batting and backing edges even with the quilted top.

Step 3. Prepare 9½ yards green zebra print binding and bind edges of quilt to finish.

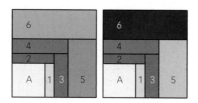

FIGURE 3 Complete blocks as shown.

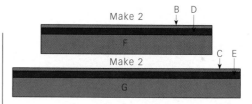

FIGURE 4 Join strips as shown to make border strips.

FIGURE 5 Sew a Half Log Cabin block to the end of each strip.

Baby Steps

Stitch and quilt one large Log Cabin block all at once to make a quick baby quilt.

PROJECT SPECIFICATIONS

Skill Level: Beginner

Quilt Size: 37" x 37"

MATERIALS

- 4½" x 4½" square pink print 1 (P1)
- 2 (4½" x 4½") squares blue print 1 (B1)
- 1 fat quarter each blue prints 2 and 3 (B2 and B3)
- 1 fat quarter each pink prints 2 and 3 (P2 and P3)
- ⅓ yard each pink prints 4 and 5 (P4 and P5) and blue print 4 (B4)
- Backing 43" x 43"
- Batting 43" x 43"
- All-purpose thread to match backing and neutral color
- Basting spray
- Basic sewing tools and supplies and sewing-machine walking foot or even-feed foot

INSTRUCTIONS

Step 1. Cut fabrics into 4½" by fabric width strips; subcut strips into the lengths as listed in **Figure 1** for each piece.

Step 2. Spray-baste the batting to the prepared backing referring to manufacturer's instructions.

Step 3. Replace your machine's presser foot with the walking foot or even-feed presser foot. Fill the bobbin with all-purpose thread to match backing fabric; thread the top of the machine with a neutral color.

Step 4. Center the P1 patch, right side up, on top of the batting and backing layers; measure

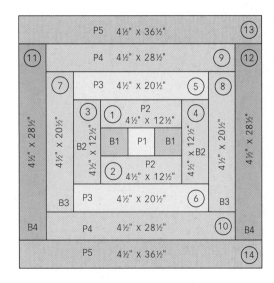

FIGURE 1 Cut fabric pieces in sizes shown; stitch in place in numerical order.

to be sure it is centered. **Note:** *If this piece is not perfectly centered, when stitching is complete, the edge pieces might not lie on the batting/backing layers.*

Step 5. Place one B1 patch right side down on top of the first patch; pin. Position the quilt layers under the presser foot. Lower the needle slowly and reverse to bring the bobbin thread to the top.

Step 6. Hold both the thread ends to keep them from tangling as you start to sew a ¼" seam through the P1, B1, batting and backing layers.

Step 7. Open the B1 patch away from the P1 patch and finger-press along the seam. Repeat with the second B1 patch on the opposite P1 edge. Add P2 strips to opposite sides of the stitched unit. Check size of stitched unit; it should measure 12½" x 12½".

Step 8. Continue adding patches referring to Figure 1 for order of piecing, and color and size of strips. Measure several times after stitching to be sure the square shape is being maintained.

Step 9. Baste ¼" from edge of completed quilt top.

Step 10. Referring to **Figure 2**, trim batting 1" larger than the quilted top all around; trim backing 2¼" larger than quilted top all around.

Step 11. At corners, trim the backing fabric on the diagonal ¼" from corner of the batting, again referring to **Figure 2**.

Step 12. Fold quilted layers diagonally from corner to corner with backing sides together;

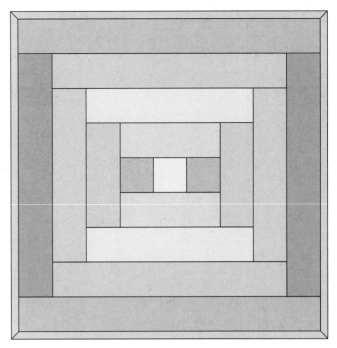

BABY STEPS Placement Diagram 37" x 37"

pin raw edges of the diagonally trimmed corner area together. Stitch from fold to outer edge of backing using a ¼" seam allowance as shown in **Figure 3**. Finger-press seam open; repeat on all corners.

Step 13. Turn stitched corners right side out over batting and quilt top; turn under ¼" along outer edge of backing. Fold backing over batting.

Step 14. Pin backing in place on quilt top, enclosing batting inside; topstitch backing edge through all layers to finish as shown in **Figure 4**. 🎁

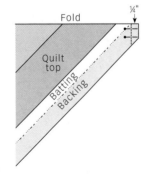

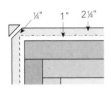

FIGURE 2 Trim batting 1" larger than the quilted top all around; trim backing 2¼" larger than quilted top all around. Trim the backing fabric on the diagonal ¼" from corner of the batting.

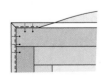

FIGURE 4 Pin backing in place on quilt top, enclosing batting inside; topstitch backing edge through all layers.

FIGURE 3 Fold quilted layers with backing fabric at corners with right sides together; pin raw edges of the diagonally trimmed area together; stitch from fold to outer edge of backing.

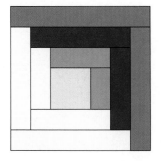

LOG CABIN
7" x 7" Block

Pink Dogwood Trails

Plain strips and Log Cabin blocks are accented by appliquéd flowers and leaves to make this pretty quilt with a springtime look.

PROJECT SPECIFICATIONS
Skill Level: Intermediate
Quilt Size: 62½" x 48½"
Block Size: 7" x 7"
Number of Blocks: 36

MATERIALS
- 1 fat quarter pink solid for flowers
- ¼ yard dark green tone-on-tone for leaves
- ⅜ yard light green tone-on-tone (A)
- ½ yard dark green tone-on-tone (B)
- ½ yard medium green solid
- ⅝ yard gold mottled
- ⅔ yard medium green mottled (C)
- 1⅓ yards cream-on-cream print
- Backing 69" x 56"
- Batting 69" x 56"
- All-purpose thread to match fabrics and brown fusible bias tape
- Quilting thread
- Yellow and brown 6-strand embroidery floss
- 1 package brown ¼" fusible bias tape
- 3 packages green double-fold bias binding

- 1 yard fusible transfer web
- Basic sewing tools and supplies

INSTRUCTIONS
Making Log Cabin Blocks
Step 1. Cut three 2½" by fabric width strips gold mottled; subcut strips into 2½" square segments for piece 1. You will need 36 squares.

Step 2. Cut two 7½" x 42½" D strips cream-on-cream print along length of fabric; set aside. Cut remaining fabric width into 1½" strips.

Step 3. Cut the A, B and C green fabrics into 1½" by fabric width strips.

Step 4. Complete 36 Log Cabin blocks beginning with the piece 1 squares and adding fabric strips referring to **Figure 1** for number and fabric order, and to

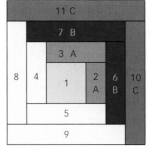

FIGURE 1 Stitch Log Cabin blocks as shown.

page 9–11 for instructions.

Step 5. When blocks are complete, press and square up to 7½" x 7½".

Completing the Top

Step 1. Join six Log Cabin blocks to make a row as shown in **Figure 2**; repeat for six block rows. Press seams in one direction.

Step 2. Join two rows as shown in **Figure 3**; press seams in one direction.

Step 3. Join the block rows with the D strips as shown in **Figure 4**; press seams toward D.

Step 4. Cut two lengths each 4", 6" and 49" and four each 5" and 7" brown ¼" fusible bias for stems.

Step 5. Mark a curving line on each D piece referring to **Figure 5** for measurement suggestions.

Step 6. Arrange the brown ¼" fusible bias pieces on the marked lines, again referring to **Figure 5**; fuse in place beginning with the shorter pieces, tucking the ends under the longer pieces and extending into seam allowance at top and bottom edges. Machine-blindstitch in place using brown all-purpose thread in the top of the machine and in the bobbin.

Step 7. Cut and piece two 1¾" x 56½" E strips and two 1¾" x 45" F strips yellow mottled. Sew E to the top and bottom and F to opposite sides of the pieced center; press seams toward strips.

Step 8. Cut and piece two 2½" x 59" G strips and two 2½" x 49" H strips medium green solid.

PINK DOGWOOD TRAILS Placement Diagram 62½" x 48½"

Sew G to the top and bottom and H to opposite sides of the pieced center; press seams toward strips.

Step 9. Prepare templates for flower and leaf shapes. Bond fusible web to the wrong side of the pink solid and dark green tone-on-tone appliqué fabrics.

Step 10. Trace shapes onto the paper side of the fused fabrics as directed on patterns for number to cut; cut out shapes on traced lines. Remove paper backing.

Step 11. Arrange 28 leaf shapes each along the stitched stems referring to the Placement Diagram for positioning; fuse in place.

Step 12. Arrange six flower shapes on each D piece at the ends of the stems; fuse shapes in place.

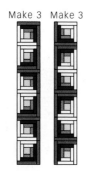

Make 3   Make 3

FIGURE 2 Join 6 Log Cabin blocks to make a row.

FIGURE 3 Join 2 rows.

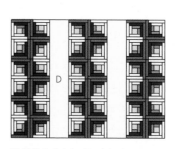

FIGURE 4 Join the block rows with the D strips.

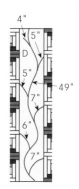

FIGURE 5 Mark lines for stems on D strips. Arrange the stem pieces on the marked lines.

FLOWER
Cut 12 pink solid

French Knot

LEAF
Cut 56 dark green
tone-on-tone

Step 13. Using all-purpose thread to match leaf and flower fabrics, machine zigzag-stitch around each fused shape.

Step 14. Using 3 strands yellow embroidery floss, make seven French knots in the center of each flower.

Step 15. Add tips to flowers using 2 strands brown embroidery floss and a satin stitch and referring to the pattern for placement.

Finishing the Quilt

Step 1. Prepare quilt top for quilting and quilt.

Step 2. When quilting is complete, trim batting and backing edges even with quilted top.

Step 3. Bind edges of quilt using green double-fold bias binding to finish. 🏠

A Log Cabin quilt starts in the center of each block. The added strips create a frame or window with the focus remaining on the center view.

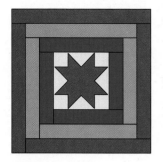

LOG CABIN STAR
15" x 15" Block

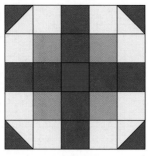

NINE-PATCH CROSS
15" x 15" Block

DESIGN > JUDITH SANDSTROM

Framed Stars

Log Cabin strips make the perfect frame for blocks with appliquéd centers. The addition of a second block helps enlarge the quilt and adds interest to the design.

PROJECT SPECIFICATIONS

Skill Level: Beginner
Quilt Size: 88" x 103"
Block Size: 15" x 15"
Number of Blocks: 30

MATERIALS

- 1¾ yards turquoise print
- 1¾ yards orange tone-on-tone
- 2 yards cream tone-on-tone
- 3 yards coordinating border stripe
- 3⅜ yards brown mottled
- Backing 94" x 109"
- Batting 94" x 109"
- Neutral color all-purpose thread
- Quilting thread
- 1 yard fusible web
- 1 yard fabric stabilizer
- Basic sewing tools and supplies

INSTRUCTIONS

Making Nine-Patch Cross Blocks

Step 1. Cut 12 brown mottled, 10 cream tone-on-tone, six orange tone-on-tone and two turquoise print 3½" by fabric width strips.

Step 2. Sew a brown mottled strip between two cream tone-on-tone strips with right sides together along length; press seams toward darker fabric. Repeat for five strip sets.

Step 3. Subcut strip sets into 3½" segments for A as shown in **Figure 1**; you will need 60 A segments.

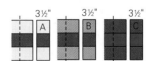

FIGURE 1 Subcut strip sets into 3½" segments to make A, B and C units.

Step 4. Sew a brown mottled strip between two orange tone-on-tone strips with right sides together along length; press seams toward darker fabric. Repeat for three strip sets.

Step 5. Subcut strip sets into 3½" segments for B, again referring to **Figure 1**; you will need 30 B segments.

Step 6. Sew a turquoise print strip between two brown mottled strips with right sides together along length; press seams toward darker fabric. Repeat for two strip sets.

Step 7. Subcut strip sets into 3½" segments for C, again referring to **Figure 1**; you will need 15 C segments.

Step 8. Cut three strips each brown mottled and cream tone-on-tone 3⅞" by fabric width; subcut strips into thirty 3⅞" squares for D. Cut each square on one diagonal to make 60 each brown mottled and cream tone-on-tone D triangles.

Step 9. Sew a brown mottled D to a cream tone-on-tone D on the diagonal to make a D unit as shown in **Figure 2**; repeat for 60 D units.

Step 10. To piece one block, join two B units with one C unit as shown in Figure 3; press seams in one direction.

Step 11. Sew an A unit to opposite sides of the B-C unit as shown in **Figure 4**; press seams toward A.

Step 12. Sew a D unit to each end of two A units as shown in **Figure 5**; press seams toward the A units. Repeat for two units. Sew an A-D unit to opposite sides of the A-B-C unit to complete one Nine-Patch Cross block as shown in **Figure 6**; repeat for 15 blocks.

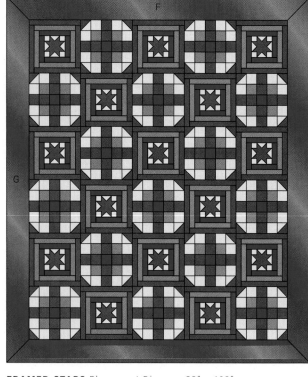

FRAMED STARS Placement Diagram 88" x 103"

Making Log Cabin Star Blocks

Step 1. Cut 23 strips brown mottled, 19 strips orange tone-on-tone and 14 strips turquoise print 2" by fabric width for log strips.

Step 2. Iron the fusible web to the wrong side of the remaining brown mottled referring to manufacturer's instructions. Prepare template for the star shape using pattern given; trace shape onto the paper side of the fused fabric referring to the pattern for number to cut.

Step 3. Cut out star shapes on traced lines; remove paper backing.

Step 4. Cut three 6½" by fabric width strips cream tone-on-tone; subcut strips into fifteen 6½" square segments for E.

FIGURE 2
Make a D unit as shown.

FIGURE 3
Join 2 B units with 1 C unit.

FIGURE 4 Sew an A unit to opposite sides of the B-C unit.

FIGURE 5 Sew a D unit to each end of an A unit.

FIGURE 6 Sew an A-D unit to opposite sides of the A-B-C unit to complete 1 Nine-Patch Cross block.

Step 5. Center a star shape on each E square referring to block drawing for positioning of star; fuse in place.

Step 6. Cut 15 squares fabric stabilizer 6" x 6"; pin a square to the wrong side of each fused E square.

Step 7. Using thread to match star shape, machine zigzag-stitch around each fused shape. When stitching is complete, remove fabric stabilizer.

Step 8. Beginning with the turquoise print strips, sew strips to the sides of the E square in numerical order referring to **Figure 7** for positioning of strips and to page 9–11 for basic instructions.

Step 9. Continue adding orange tone-on-tone and brown mottled strips to the framed center square, again referring to Figure 7 for order of stitching.

Step 10. Measure and trim blocks to 15½" x 15½" to complete.

Completing the Top

Step 1. Join two Nine-Patch Cross blocks with three Log Cabin Star blocks to make a row referring to the Placement Diagram for positioning of blocks; repeat for three rows. Press seams toward Log Cabin Star blocks.

Step 2. Join two Log Cabin Star blocks with three Nine-Patch Cross blocks to make a row, again referring to the Placement Diagram for positioning of blocks; repeat for three rows. Press seams toward Log Cabin Star blocks.

Step 3. Join the rows referring to the Placement Diagram for positioning; press seams in one direction.

Step 4. Cut two identical 7" x 90" F strips and two identical 7" x 105" G strips along the length of the coordinating border stripe.

Step 5. Center and sew an F strip to the top and bottom and a G strip to each long side mitering corners; trim excess seam to ¼". Press seams open.

Finishing the Quilt

Step 1. Prepare quilt top for quilting and quilt.

Step 2. When quilting is complete, trim batting and backing edges even with quilted top.

Step 3. Prepare 11 yards turquoise print binding and bind edges of quilt to finish. 🏠

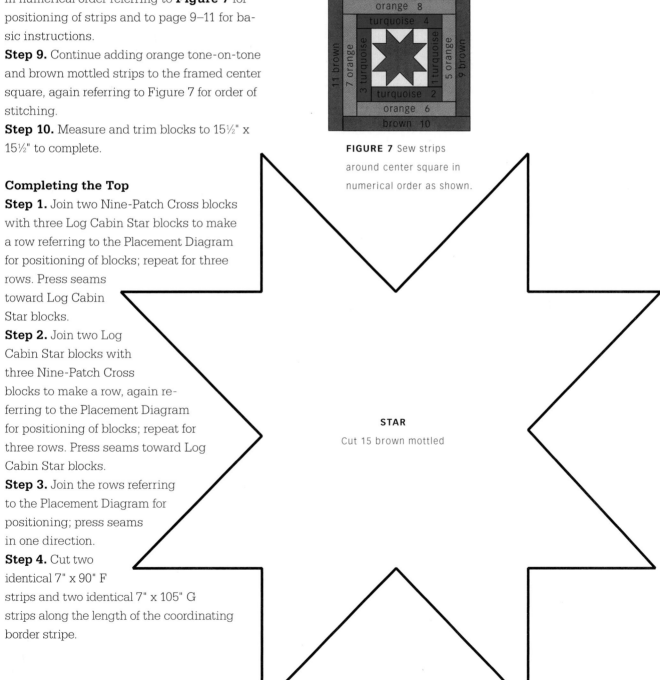

FIGURE 7 Sew strips around center square in numerical order as shown.

STAR
Cut 15 brown mottled

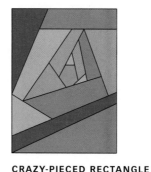

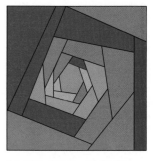

CRAZY-PIECED RECTANGLE
12" x 16" Block

CRAZY-PIECED SQUARE
16" x 16" Block

DESIGN > FRIEDA L. ANDERSON

Shimmering Foliage

The design was based on the designer's daily walks in the woods with her dog George.

LEAF
12" x 16" Block

PROJECT NOTES

The Leaf blocks in the center section of the quilt are strip-pieced using gradations of hand-dyed greens. The leaves are framed with bright orange to show the contrast between spring and fall that appears naturally as the seasons change. The border is made with blocks that are crazy-pieced on a paper foundation using hand-dyed shades of fuchsia, reflecting the crazy effect fallen leaves make on the ground. The hand-dyed fabrics appear to vary in color enough to add shading to the leaves and crazy-pieced border blocks.

I hand-dyed the fabrics using Kona cotton for the base fabric and Procion MX dyes—fuchsia with degrees of better black, lemon yellow with degrees of better black, purple-with-black, and orange to achieve the colors.

PROJECT SPECIFICATIONS

Skill Level: Advanced
Quilt Size: 88" x 88"
Block Size: 12" x 16" and 16" x 16"
Number of Blocks: 8, 12 and 16

MATERIALS

- ⅙ yard hand-dyed purple
- 1 yard fuchsia solid for binding
- 4 yards hand-dyed bright orange
- 4–6 yards total hand-dyed gradients of green
- 4–6 yards total hand-dyed gradients of fuchsia
- Backing 94" x 94"
- Batting 94" x 94"
- All-purpose thread to match fabrics
- Quilting thread
- 1 roll of newsprint
- Basic sewing tools and supplies and a 30-degree-angle ruler, glue stick and plastic bags

INSTRUCTIONS

Piecing Leaf Blocks

Step 1. Free-form cut (without a ruler) the green fabrics into strips varying 1" to 2" wide and 9" long. Randomly select different colors and sizes and sew together 12–15 strips to make a unit. Repeat for 32 units.

Step 2. Prepare a newsprint foundation pattern 14" tall and 3½"–5" wide at the widest point to make a leaf shape as shown in

Figure 1; repeat to make 16 leaf patterns, making several different shapes and sizes.

Step 3. Mark a 30-degree-angled line on 16 patterns using the angled ruler as shown in **Figure 2**. Repeat to mark a line on the opposite side of the patterns for reverse pieces.

Step 4. Place a leaf pattern on top of one strip unit, aligning 30-degree-angle line on pattern with seam line on unit as shown in **Figure 3**. Cut out leaf shape ¼" beyond edge of pattern all around. Turn pattern over and place on another strip unit; cut out a reversed leaf shape. Repeat for 16 leaves and 16 reversed leaves.

Step 5. Cut 32 bright orange rectangles 8" x 17".

Step 6. Align the straight edge of the leaf halves on one long edge of each rectangle referring to **Figure 4**.

Step 7. Turn under curved edges of leaf shapes and hand-appliqué in place; cut away orange fabric beneath the appliqué shape.

Step 8. Cut a 2" x 16" strip of fuchsia. Using a ¼" seam allowance, sew the strip to one appliquéd leaf unit, with end of strip aligned with edge of rectangle on the bottom leaf end and

SHIMMERING FOLIAGE Placement Diagram 88" x 88"

leaving about a 2" space at the top leaf end as shown in **Figure 5**; press seam toward strip.

Step 9. Using a ruler, create a wedge shape from fuchsia, ending in a point at the top and about ¾" wide at the bottom. Sew a reversed leaf half to the strip with the strip on top, tapering to the pointed end of the strip until stitching meets the previously stitched seam. Stop and secure stitching; fold seam allowance of top leaf rectangle up, begin stitching at secured point and continue to end of rectangle to create a disappearing point as shown in Figure 6; press seams toward strip.

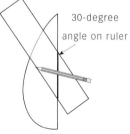

FIGURE 1 Prepare a pattern 14" tall and 3½"–5" wide at the widest point to make a leaf shape.

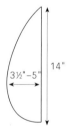

FIGURE 3 Align seam line of green strip with angled line on pattern.

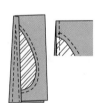

FIGURE 6 Taper seam at the narrow end until stitching meets the previously stitched seam.

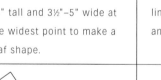

FIGURE 2 Mark a 30-degree angled-line on each pattern.

FIGURE 4 Align the straight edge of 1 leaf on a rectangle.

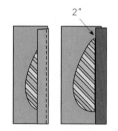

FIGURE 5 Sew the strip to 1 appliquéd leaf unit, with 1 end of strip aligned with edge of rectangle on the bottom leaf end and leaving about a 2" space at the top leaf end.

FIGURE 7 Randomly cut 6-sided center pieces about 3" in size.

Note: *Don't worry if the leaf strips don't match up side to side; this creates movement and excitement.* Press blocks; trim to 12½" x 16½".

Piecing the Crazy-Patch Blocks

Step 1. Cut eight newsprint paper foundations 13" x 17" and twelve 17" x 17". Fold each paper foundation to find the center.

Step 2. Using leftover orange scraps, randomly cut 20 six-sided center pieces about 3" in size as shown in **Figure 7**.

Step 3. Using a glue stick, glue an orange center piece over the center of each paper shape.

Step 4. Separate the fuchsia fabrics from lightest to darkest. **Note:** *The sample has six different shades.*

Step 5. Randomly cut each fabric into 2"–3½" by fabric width strips and place in plastic bags numbered to correspond to the value of fabric.

Step 6. Starting with the lightest and working your way out to the darkest, with right side against the center piece, sew a strip to the foundation; press to the right side and trim as shown in **Figure 8**. Repeat with strips around the center to fill foundation, saving the darkest two fabrics for the last rounds of piecing. Trim strip ends as you stitch; square up the foundation pieces to 16½" x 16½" and 12½" x 16½" when crazy-patchwork is complete.

Completing the Top

Step 1. Cut four 4½" x 4½" squares purple.

Step 2. Sew one Leaf block to a square, stopping stitching 1" from bottom of seam as shown in **Figure 9**.

Step 3. Sew a second leaf block to the completed seam side of the stitched unit as shown in **Figure 10**; press seam toward Leaf block.

Step 4. Add two more Leaf blocks, completing first unstitched seam when adding the last block as shown in **Figure 11**. Press seams toward Leaf blocks. Repeat for four Leaf-block units.

Step 5. Join two Leaf-block units to make a row referring to the Placement Diagram for positioning of the units; repeat for two rows. Press seams in opposite directions. Join the rows; press seam in one direction.

Step 6. Join two Crazy-Pieced Squares with two Crazy-Pieced Rectangles to make a side row as shown in **Figure 12**; press seams in one direction. Repeat for two side rows. Sew a side row to opposite sides of the pieced center; press seams toward side rows.

Step 7. Join two Crazy-Pieced Rectangles with four Crazy-Pieced Squares to make a top row; repeat for bottom row. Press seams in one direction.

Step 8. Sew the pieced rows to the top and bottom of the pieced section to complete the pieced top; press seams toward rows.

Step 9. Remove all paper foundations.

Finishing the Quilt

Step 1. Prepare quilt top for quilting and quilt.

Step 2. When quilting is complete, trim batting and backing edges even with the quilted top.

Step 3. Prepare 10⅜ yards fuchsia binding and bind edges of quilt to finish. 🧰

FIGURE 8 Sew strip to the foundation; press to the right side and trim.

FIGURE 9 Sew a Leaf block to a square, stopping stitching 1" from bottom of seam.

FIGURE 10 Sew a second leaf block to the completed seam side of the stitched unit.

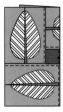

FIGURE 11 Complete unstitched seam when adding last block.

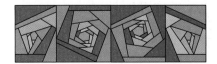

FIGURE 12 Join 2 Crazy-Pieced Squares with 2 Crazy-Pieced Rectangles to make a side row.

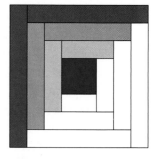

LOG CABIN
5" x 5" Block

DESIGN > MARIAN SHENK

Delft
Cabins

Blue and white fabrics combine to create a Log Cabin quilt with the look of Dutch china.

PROJECT SPECIFICATIONS

Skill Level: Intermediate

Quilt Size: 34" x 34"

Block Size: 5" x 5"

Number of Blocks: 12

MATERIALS

- Scrap pale blue solid
- ¼ yard medium blue mottled (B)
- 1 fat quarter royal blue solid
- ⅜ yard light blue tone-on-tone (A)
- ½ yard dark blue tone-on-tone (C)
- ⅝ yard royal blue mottled
- 1 yard white-on-white print
- Backing 40" x 40"
- Batting 40" x 40"
- All-purpose thread to match fabrics and navy narrow bias tape
- Quilting thread
- 1 package navy narrow bias tape
- Basic sewing tools and supplies

INSTRUCTIONS
Making Log Cabin Blocks

Step 1. Cut one 1¾" by fabric width strip royal blue solid; subcut strip into 1¾" square segments for piece 1. You will need 12 squares.

Step 2. Prepare template for D using pattern given; cut as directed on the piece. Set aside.

Step 3. Cut eight white-on-white print, two light blue A, three medium blue B and four dark blue C 1⅛" by fabric width strips for logs.

Step 4. Complete 12 Log Cabin blocks beginning with the piece 1 squares and adding fabric strips referring to **Figure 1** for number and fabric order and to page 9–11 for instructions.

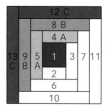

FIGURE 1 Stitch Log Cabin blocks as shown.

Step 5. When blocks are complete, press and square up to 5½" x 5½".

Completing the Center Appliqué Square

Step 1. Cut a 12¾" x 12¾" square white-on-white print for E. Fold the square and crease to mark horizontal, vertical and diagonal centers.

Step 2. Prepare templates for each appliqué shape using the full-size motif given; cut as directed for each piece, adding a ¼" seam allowance when cutting for hand appliqué.

Step 3. Trace the full-size motif on E using diagonal crease lines as guides for placement, tracing a motif on each diagonal corner with the circle in the center of E.

Step 4. Turn under seam allowance on all appliqué pieces; baste in place.

Step 5. Cut four 5½" lengths navy narrow bias tape for stems.

Step 6. Beginning with the stem pieces, arrange and baste pieces in place on E; hand-stitch in place using thread to match fabrics.

Step 7. Cut two 1½" x 12¾" F strips and two 1½" x 14¾" G strips royal blue solid. Sew F to opposite sides and G to the top and bottom of the appliquéd E square; press seams toward strips.

Completing the Top

Step 1. Join three Log Cabin blocks, two royal blue mottled D and four white-on-white print D triangles to make a side unit as shown in **Figure 2**; repeat for four side units. Press seams in one direction.

DELFT CABINS Placement Diagram 34" x 34"

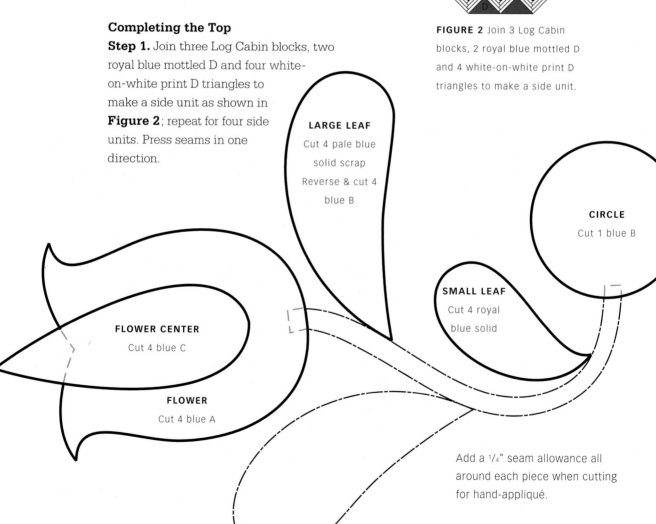

FIGURE 2 Join 3 Log Cabin blocks, 2 royal blue mottled D and 4 white-on-white print D triangles to make a side unit.

LARGE LEAF
Cut 4 pale blue
solid scrap
Reverse & cut 4
blue B

CIRCLE
Cut 1 blue B

SMALL LEAF
Cut 4 royal
blue solid

FLOWER CENTER
Cut 4 blue C

FLOWER
Cut 4 blue A

Add a ¼" seam allowance all
around each piece when cutting
for hand-appliqué.

Step 2. Sew a side unit to each side of the ap-pliquéd center, stitching side seams first and then corner seams. The pieced unit should measure 29" x 29" at this point.

Step 3. Cut two 1¾" x 29" H strips and two 1¾" x 31½" I strips blue A. Sew H to oppo-site sides and I to the top and bottom of the pieced section; press seams toward strips.

Step 4. Cut two 2" x 31½" J strips and two 2" x 34½" strips blue C. Sew J to opposite sides and K to the top and bottom of the pieced sec-tion; press seams toward strips.

Finishing the Quilt

Step 1. Prepare quilt top for quilting and quilt.

Step 2. When quilting is complete, trim bat-ting and backing edges even with quilted top.

Step 3. Prepare 4⅛ yards royal blue mottled binding and bind edges of quilt to finish. 🏠

D

Cut 8 royal blue mottled & 16 white-on-white print

Adding a View

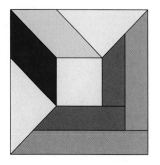

FLOWER
6" x 6" Block

Stained Glass
Star Flower

Use narrow black bias tape to frame triangles in rounds to create a Log Cabin look.

PROJECT SPECIFICATIONS

Skill Level: Advanced
Quilt Size: 39½" x 39½"
Block Size: 6" x 6"
Number of Blocks: 4

MATERIALS

- 5" x 5" scrap yellow mottled
- 6" x 12" scrap each light and dark green solids
- ⅛ yard light lavender dot
- ¼ yard dark purple print
- ¼ yard mauve print
- ⅜ yard purple solid
- ⅝ yard lavender mottled
- ⅝ yard purple print
- 1 yard gray floral tone-on-tone
- Backing 46" x 46"
- Batting 46" x 46"
- All-purpose thread to match fabrics and fusible bias
- Quilting thread
- 15 yards black ¼"-wide fusible bias
- 2 packages black wide bias binding
- Basting spray
- Basic sewing tools and supplies

INSTRUCTIONS

Completing the Quilt Center

Step 1. Prepare templates for pieces E–K using patterns given; cut as directed on each piece.

Step 2. To piece one block, sew H to one side of E as shown in **Figure 1**; add I to the adjacent side.

Step 3. Sew J to the H side and K to the I side to complete half the block referring to **Figure 2**. Press seams away from E as pieces are added.

Step 4. Sew F to G and FR to G, and join the units as shown in **Figure 3**; press seams toward G.

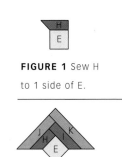

FIGURE 1 Sew H to 1 side of E.

FIGURE 2 Complete half the block as shown.

FIGURE 3 Sew F to G and FR to G and join the units as shown.

Step 5. Sew the F-G unit to the previously pieced unit as shown in **Figure 4** to complete one Flower block. Press seams away from E. Repeat for four blocks.

Step 6. Cut one strip lavender mottled and two strips purple print 1½" by fabric width. Sew the lavender mottled strip between the two purple print strips with right sides together along length. Press seams in one direction.

Step 7. Subcut strip set into four 6½" M segments as shown in **Figure 5**.

Step 8. Cut one 3½" x 3½" L square yellow mottled.

Step 9. Join two Flower blocks with M as shown in **Figure 6**; press seams toward M. Repeat for two units.

Step 10. Join two M units with L as shown in **Figure 7**; press seams toward M.

Step 11. Join the pieced units as shown in **Figure 8**; press seams toward M-L.

Step 12. Cut two 1" x 15½" V strips and two 1" x 16½" W strips purple solid. Sew V to opposite sides and W to the top and bottom of the pieced unit to complete the quilt center.

Completing the Top

Step 1. Cut two 8" x 16½" N strips and two 8" x 31½" O strips gray floral tone-on-tone.

Step 2. Sew N to opposite sides and O to the top and bottom of the quilt center as shown in **Figure 9**; press seams toward N and O.

Step 3. Prepare templates for pieces A–D us-

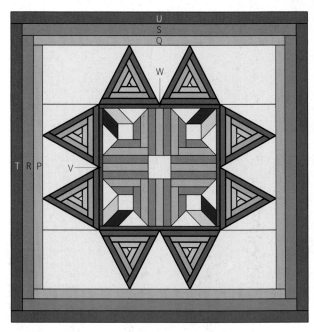

STAINED GLASS STAR FLOWER Placement Diagram 39½" x 39½"

ing full-size pattern given. Cut as directed on each piece.

Step 4. Apply basting spray to the wrong side of each piece.

Step 5. Place two D pieces on N ⅛" from V strip and ¼" apart at bottom edges as shown in Figure 10. Repeat to place two D pieces on each N strip and two on each O strip.

Step 6. Apply C, B and finally A to each D piece referring to full-size pattern for placement.

Step 7. Referring to the full-size bias-appliqué pattern, apply ¼"-wide fusible bias to layered triangle units centering bias over edges of fabric triangles and aligning with N-V or

FIGURE 9 Sew N to opposite sides and O to the top and bottom of the quilt center.

FIGURE 4 Sew the F-G unit to the previously pieced unit.

FIGURE 5 Subcut strip set into 6½" M segments.

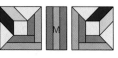

FIGURE 6 Join 2 Flower blocks with M.

FIGURE 7 Join 2 M units with L.

FIGURE 8 Join the pieced units.

FIGURE 10 Place 2 D pieces on N.

O-W seams at bottom edge. Turn under ends of the bottom (12) strip at an angle to match with angled side edges. Fuse in place; machine-stitch both edges of each piece using matching all-purpose thread. Trim top point even with edges of N or O border strip.

Step 8. Cut two strips each 1¾" x 31½" (P) and 1¾" x 34" (Q) lavender mottled. Sew P to opposite sides and Q to the top and bottom of the quilt center; press seams toward P and Q.

Step 9. Cut two strips each 2" x 34" (R) and 2" x 37" (S) purple print. Sew R to opposite sides and S to the top and bottom of the quilt center; press seams toward R and S.

Step 10. Cut two strips each 2" x 37" (T) and 2" x 40" (U) purple solid. Sew T to opposite sides and U to the top and bottom of the quilt center; press seams toward T and U.

Finishing the Quilt

Step 1. Prepare quilt top for quilting and quilt.

Step 2. When quilting is complete, trim batting and backing edges even with the quilted top.

Step 3. Bind edges with black wide bias binding to finish.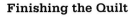

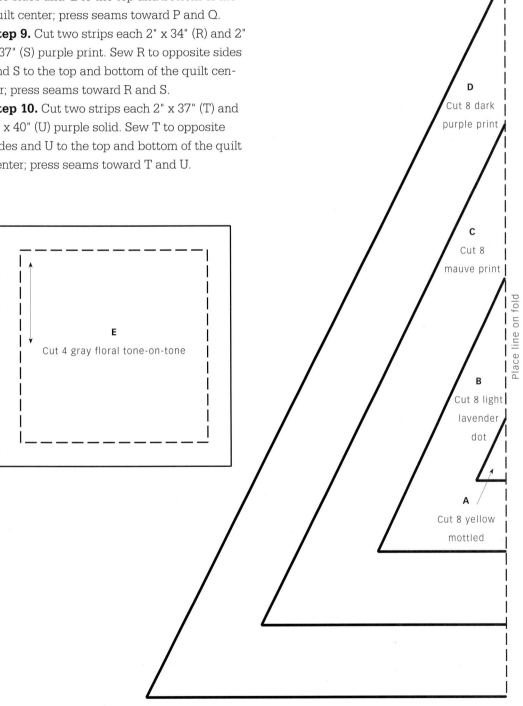

E
Cut 4 gray floral tone-on-tone

D
Cut 8 dark purple print

C
Cut 8 mauve print

B
Cut 8 light lavender dot

A
Cut 8 yellow mottled

Place line on fold

Adding a View

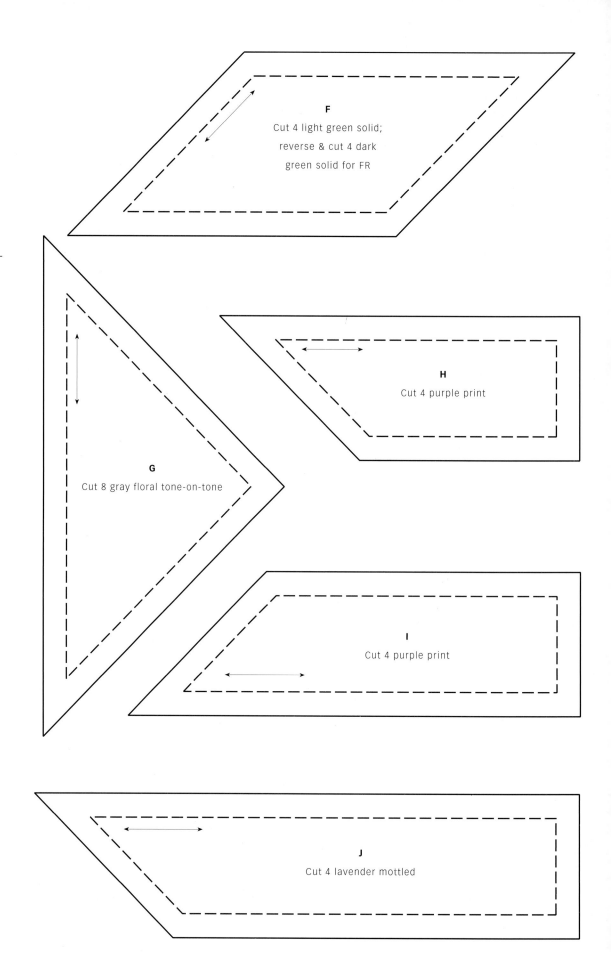

F
Cut 4 light green solid;
reverse & cut 4 dark
green solid for FR

G
Cut 8 gray floral tone-on-tone

H
Cut 4 purple print

I
Cut 4 purple print

J
Cut 4 lavender mottled

BIAS-APPLIQUE PATTERN

Center bias over edges of triangles

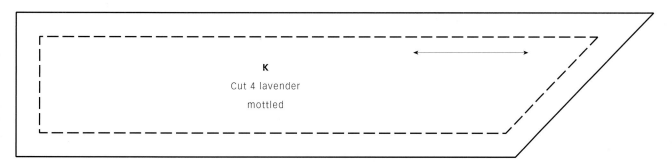

K

Cut 4 lavender

mottled

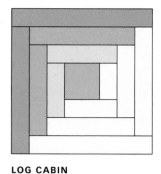

LOG CABIN
8" x 8" Block

Cabins Around the Posy

The light areas of the Log Cabin blocks make the perfect appliqué background for pretty floral designs.

PROJECT SPECIFICATIONS

Skill Level: Intermediate
Quilt Size: 38½" x 38½"
Block Size: 8" x 8"
Number of Blocks: 16

MATERIALS

- Scraps green tone-on-tone and light blue mottled
- ¼ yard light peach mottled (A)
- ⅓ yard peach solid
- ⅓ yard medium peach mottled (B)
- ⅜ yard dark peach tone-on-tone (C)
- ½ yard royal blue mottled
- ¾ yard cream-on-cream print
- Backing 44" x 44"
- Batting 44" x 44"
- All-purpose thread to match fabrics
- Quilting thread
- Green 6-strand embroidery floss
- Basic sewing tools and supplies

INSTRUCTIONS

Making Log Cabin Blocks

Step 1. Cut one 2½" by fabric width strip peach solid; subcut strip into 2½" square segments for piece 1. You will need 16 squares.

Step 2. Cut four light and six medium peach mottled, eight dark peach tone-on-tone and 13 cream-on-cream print 1½" by fabric width strips.

Step 3. Complete 16 Log Cabin blocks beginning with the piece 1 squares and adding fabric strips referring to **Figure 1** for fabric and number order and to page 9–11 for instructions.

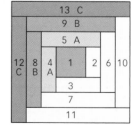

FIGURE 1 Stitch Log Cabin blocks as shown.

Step 4. When blocks are complete, press and square up to 8½" x 8½".

Completing the Top

Step 1. Join four Log Cabin blocks to make a row as shown in **Figure 2**; repeat for four rows. Press seams in one direction.

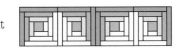

FIGURE 2 Join 4 Log Cabin blocks to make a row.

Step 2. Join rows referring to the Placement Diagram; press seams in one direction.

Step 3. Cut two 1¾" x 32½" A strips and two 1¾" x 35" B strips peach solid. Sew the A strips to opposite sides and B strips to the top and bottom of the pieced center; press seams toward strips.

Step 4. Cut two 2½" x 35" C strips and two 2½" x 39" D strips royal blue mottled. Sew the C strips to opposite sides and D strips to the

Adding a View

top and bottom of the pieced center; press seams toward strips.

Step 5. Prepare templates for each appliqué shape using the full-size motif given; cut as directed for each piece, adding a ¼" seam allowance when cutting for hand appliqué.

Step 6. Turn under seam allowance on all appliqué pieces; baste to hold.

Step 7. Arrange and baste one appliqué motif on one of the light areas of the pieced top referring to **Figure 3**.

Step 8. Stem-stitch bud stems using 3 strands green embroidery floss.

Finishing the Quilt

Step 1. Prepare quilt top for quilting and quilt, stopping quilting stitches in the ditch of the A and B strips; do not quilt in the C and D strips.

Step 2. When quilting is complete, trim batting and backing edges ¾" smaller than the quilt top all around.

Step 3. Turn under the C and D strips ¼" and turn ½" to the wrong side of the quilted top; hand-stitch in place to finish. 🏠

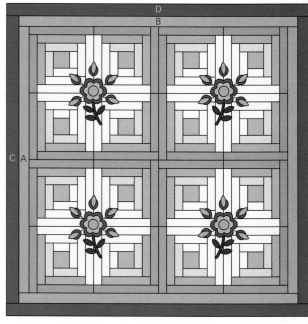

CABINS AROUND THE POSY Placement Diagram 38½" x 38½"

FIGURE 3 Arrange and baste 1 appliqué motif on 1 of the light areas of the pieced top.

Add a ¼" seam allowance all around each piece when cutting for hand-appliqué.

INNER BUD
Cut 20 medium peach mottled

INNER FLOWER
Cut 4 light blue mottled scrap

FLOWER CENTER
Cut 4 medium peach mottled

LEAF
Cut 12 green tone-on-tone scrap

STEM
Cut 4 green tone-on-tone scrap (reverse 2)

OUTER BUD
Cut 20 royal blue mottled

OUTER FLOWER
Cut 4 royal blue mottled

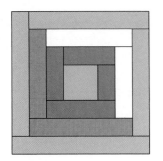

CENTER LOG
10" x 10" Block

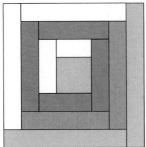

CORNER LOG
10" x 10" Block

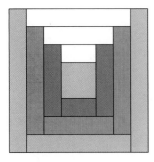

COURTHOUSE STEPS
10" x 10" Block

DESIGN > HOLLY DANIELS

Bed of Roses

The large floral print used in the quilt has a blue background and lots of flowers, but the rose is the largest—thus the name, Bed of Roses.

PROJECT SPECIFICATIONS

Skill Level: Intermediate

Quilt Size: 83" x 93"

Block Size: 10" x 10"

Number of Blocks: 44

MATERIALS

- 1¼ yards white solid
- 1¼ yards green print
- 1⅓ yards blue print
- 3 yards blue floral
- 3¼ yards pink print
- Backing 89" x 99"
- Batting 89" x 99"
- Neutral color all-purpose thread
- Quilting thread
- Basic sewing tools and supplies

INSTRUCTIONS

Making Courthouse Steps Blocks

Step 1. Cut the white solid, and green and blue prints into 1¾" by fabric width strips. In addition, cut twenty-three 1¾" by fabric width strips pink print.

Step 2. Cut the strips into 30 segments each in the following listed sizes: 3" white solid for A; 5½" white solid for E; 8" white solid for I; and 8" pink print for J.

Step 3. Cut 60 pink print segments 10½" for K and L.

Step 4. Cut blue print segments in the sizes listed: four 3" for B; thirty-four 5½" for C, D and F; and fifty-two 8" for G and H.

Step 5. Cut green print segments in the sizes listed: twenty-six 3" for B; fifty-six 5 ½" for C, D and F; and eight 8" for G and H.

Step 6. Cut four 3" by fabric width strips pink print; subcut strips into forty-four 3" squares for X. Set aside 14 X squares for Center and Corner Log Blocks.

Step 7. To make one Courthouse Steps block, sew A to one side and B to the opposite side

of X as shown in **Figure 1**; press seams away from X.

Step 8. Continue to add pieces to opposite sides of the A-B-X unit referring to **Figure 2**, pressing seams toward most recently added piece after sewing to complete one block; repeat for 26 blocks with blue print F, G and H pieces and green print B, C and D for border blocks and four blocks with reversed green and blue prints placement for center section blocks.

Making Center and Corner Blocks

Step 1. From the remaining strips cut in Step 1 for Courthouse Steps blocks, cut the following segments: 3"—10 white solid and four blue print for A; 4¼"—10 white solid and four blue print for B; 4¼"—14 blue print for C; 5½"—14 blue print for D; 5½"—10 blue print and four white solid for E; 6¾"—10 blue print and four white solid for F; 6¾"—14 green print for G; 8"—14 green print for H; 8"—10 white solid and four pink print for I; 9¼"—10 white solid and four pink print for J; 9¼"—14 pink print for K; and 10½"—14 pink print for L.

Step 2. Using pieces cut in Step 1 and previously cut X pieces, and referring to **Figures 3 and 4**, piece four Center Log blocks and 10 Corner Log blocks referring to numbers for order of piecing, and letters for color and size of strips. Press all seams toward the most recently added piece after sewing.

Step 3. Measure and trim all blocks to 10½" x 10½".

Completing the Top

Step 1. Cut one 15½" x 15½" square blue floral for M; cut the square in half on both diagonals to make M triangles. Discard two M triangles.

Step 2. Cut two 22¼" x 22¼" squares blue floral for N; cut each square in half on one diagonal to make N triangles.

Step 3. Arrange four Courthouse Steps blocks with the Center Log and Corner Log blocks, and the M and N triangles in diagonal rows as shown in **Figure 5**; join in rows. Press seams in adjacent rows in opposite directions.

Step 4. Join the rows with the M and N

FIGURE 1 Sew A to 1 side and B to the opposite side of X.

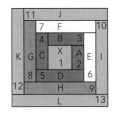

FIGURE 3 Complete 4 Center Log blocks as shown.

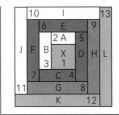

FIGURE 4 Complete 10 Corner Log blocks as shown.

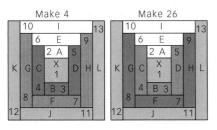

FIGURE 2 Complete 30 Courthouse Steps blocks as shown.

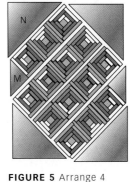

FIGURE 5 Arrange 4 Courthouse Steps blocks with the Center Log and Corner Log blocks and the M and N triangles in diagonal rows.

Adding a View

triangles to complete the pieced top; press seams toward M and N and in one direction in the center pieced area. The pieced center section should measure 43" x 57".

Step 5. Cut and piece two 2" x 57" O strips and two 2" x 46" P strips pink print. Sew O to opposite long sides and P to the top and bottom of the pieced center; press seams toward strips.

Step 6. Cut and piece two 7¾" x 60" Q strips and two 6" x 60½" R strips blue floral. Sew Q to opposite long sides and R to the top and bottom of the pieced center; press seams toward strips. The pieced section should now measure 60½" x 70½".

Step 7. Join seven Courthouse Steps blocks to make a side strip as shown in **Figure 6**; press seams in one direction. Sew a strip to opposite sides of the pieced center referring to the Placement Diagram for positioning of strips; press seams toward Q.

Step 8. Join six Courthouse Steps blocks with two Corner Log blocks to make a strip as shown in **Figure 7**; repeat for two strips. Press seams in one direction. Sew a strip to the top and bottom of the pieced center referring to the Placement Diagram for positioning of strips; press seams toward R.

Step 9. Cut and piece two 2" x 90½" S strips and two 2" x 83½" T strips pink print. Sew S to opposite long sides and T to the top and bottom of the pieced center; press seams toward strips to complete the pieced top.

BED OF ROSES Placement Diagram 83" x 93"

Finishing the Quilt

Step 1. Prepare quilt top for quilting and quilt.

Step 2. When quilting is complete, trim batting and backing edges even with the quilted top.

Step 3. Prepare 10¼ yards pink print binding and bind edges of quilt to finish. 🏠

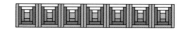

FIGURE 6 Join 7 Courthouse Steps blocks to make a side strip.

FIGURE 7 Join 6 Courthouse Steps blocks with 2 Corner Log blocks to make a strip.

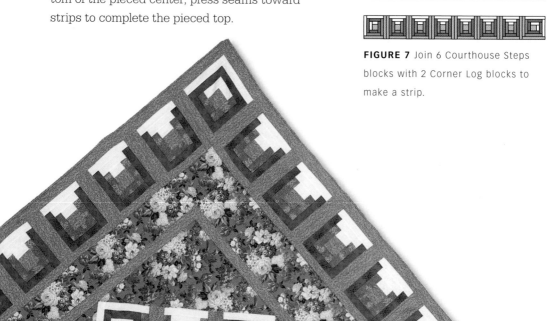

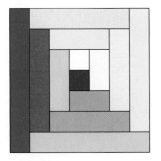

LOG CABIN

7" x 7"

Posies 'Round the Cabin

Scrappy Log Cabin blocks set in the Barn Raising pattern with appliquéd posies make up this summery-looking quilt.

PROJECT SPECIFICATIONS

Skill Level: Beginner

Quilt Size: 33" x 33"

Block Size: 7" x 7"

Number of Blocks: 16

MATERIALS

- Scraps of assorted prints in cream/tan, red, green, yellow and blue for Log Cabin blocks and appliqué (sample uses 8 prints of each color and 16 cream/tan light prints)
- Fat quarter dark green print
- ⅛ yard each green and blue prints
- ½ yard yellow print
- ⅝ yard red dot
- Backing 39" x 39"
- Batting 39" x 39"
- All-purpose thread to match appliqué fabrics
- Quilting thread
- Cardboard
- Basic sewing tools and supplies

INSTRUCTIONS

Making Log Cabin Blocks

Step 1. Cut scrap fabrics into 1½"-wide strips; cut sixteen 1½" squares red fabrics for block centers.

Step 2. Select a light strip; sew to one side of a red square; trim and press referring to page 9–11 for instructions.

Step 3. Continue to add strips in numerical order keeping lighter fabrics on two adjacent sides of the center and darker fabrics on the remaining two adjacent sides as shown in **Figure 1** to complete one block; repeat for 16 blocks.

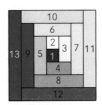

FIGURE 1 Add strips around the center in numerical order with lights and darks on opposite sides as shown.

Completing the Top

Step 1. Arrange blocks in four rows of four blocks each referring to the Placement Diagram for positioning of blocks. Join blocks in rows; press seams in one direction. Join rows; press seams in one direction.

Step 2. Prepare templates for appliqué shapes using patterns given. Cut as directed on each piece, adding a ¼" seam all around when cutting for seam allowance.

Step 3. Cut a circle piece for each size flower center from cardboard. Hand-stitch all around

fabric circles ⅛" from edge.

Step 4. Place a small fabric circle on the small cardboard circle; pull thread to gather fabric around cardboard. Press well using the tip of the iron around edge. Clip stitching and carefully remove cardboard; press again. Repeat for all large and small flower center circles.

Step 5. Cut four 1" x 15" strips on the bias of the dark green print. Fold each strip in half along length with wrong sides together. Sew long raw edges together ¼" from edge. Trim seams to a scant ⅛"; refold the strip, centering the stitched seam on the backside; press.

Step 6. Prepare flower and leaf shapes for hand appliqué using your preferred method.

Step 7. Referring to the Placement Diagram, arrange the prepared appliqué shapes on the pieced top with small blue flowers at each outer corner, and large red flowers at midpoint on each side. Curve and place each bias vine so it reaches from one large flower to the next; trim as necessary and tuck the ends under the edge of flower petals. Place a small red flower midway between the large flowers. Arrange two leaves around each flower, placing small leaves with small flowers and large leaves with large flowers. Pin all appliqué pieces in place; hand-stitch to top with all-purpose thread to match appliqué fabrics.

Step 8. Cut two 3" x 28½" A strips and two 3" x 33½" B strips red dot. Sew A to opposite sides and B to the top and bottom of the completed center; press seams toward strips.

Finishing the Quilt

Step 1. Prepare quilt top for quilting and quilt.

Step 2. When quilting is complete, trim batting

POSIES 'ROUND THE CABIN Placement Diagram 33" x 33"

and backing edges even with the quilted top.

Step 3. Prepare 4 yards yellow print binding and bind edges of quilt to finish. 🏠

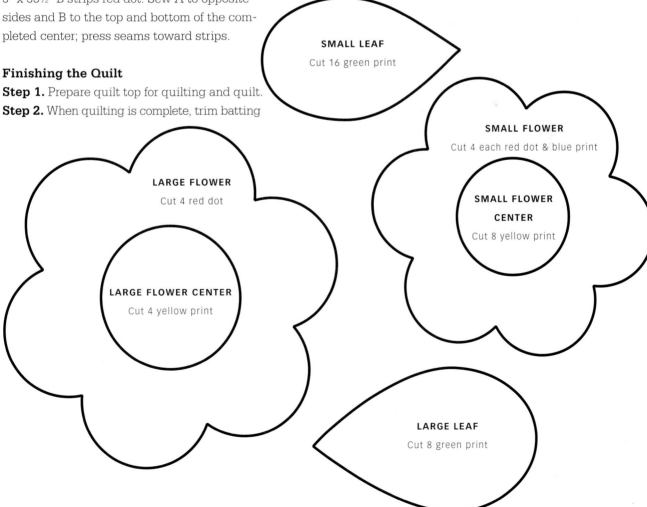

SMALL LEAF
Cut 16 green print

SMALL FLOWER
Cut 4 each red dot & blue print

SMALL FLOWER CENTER
Cut 8 yellow print

LARGE FLOWER
Cut 4 red dot

LARGE FLOWER CENTER
Cut 4 yellow print

LARGE LEAF
Cut 8 green print

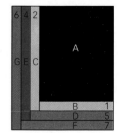

LOG CABIN

11" x 13" Block

Log Cabin
Stable

Make this wall quilt for the horse lover in your family.

PROJECT SPECIFICATIONS

Skill Level: Intermediate

Quilt Size: 43" x 31½"

Block Size: 11" x 13"

Number of Blocks: 3

MATERIALS

- 3" x 6" scrap of brown mottled
- 1 fat quarter each 3 red prints
- 1 yard wood-grain print
- ¼ yard blue sky print
- ¼ yard each gray and cream faux suede or velour
- ⅓ yard black solid
- ½ yard dark red solid
- Backing 49" x 38"
- Batting 49" x 38"
- Neutral color all-purpose thread
- 6-strand dark brown embroidery floss
- Quilting thread
- 1 yard 4"-long cream fringe
- 1⅜ yards ¼"-wide red ribbon
- 6 (½") metal buttons
- 5 (¾") wood-look buttons
- 3" x 6" scrap of fusible web
- Basic sewing tools and supplies

INSTRUCTIONS

Making Pieced Top

Step 1. Cut three rectangles 8½" x 10½" black solid for A.

Step 2. Cut the following strips along the length of the wood-grain print: three 1½" x 8½" for B, three 1½" x 11½" for C, one 3½" x 33½" for J, two 2½" x 33½" for K and two 2½" x 26" for L.

Step 3. From the red print fat quarters, cut three strips each of the following sizes: 1½" x 9½" for D, 1½" x 10½" for F, 1½" x 12½" for E and 1½" x 13½" for G. **Note:** *Cut strips randomly from all the red prints to add variety to the blocks.*

Step 4. Cut two strips each 3½" x 37½" for M and 3½" x 32" for N from dark red solid.

Step 5. Prepare templates for H and I using patterns given; cut as directed for H and I.

Step 6. Sew B–G strips to one A rectangle to complete one block as shown in **Figure 1**; press seams toward

FIGURE 1 Join strips with A as shown to make Log Cabin block.

strips. Repeat for three Log Cabin blocks.

Step 7. Join blocks on long sides to make a row referring to **Figure 2**; press seams in one direction.

Step 8. Add J to the top of the block row and K to the bottom, again referring to **Figure 2**.

Step 9. Join H and I triangles as shown in **Figure 3** to make stable roof unit; press seams toward the red triangles.

Step 10. Sew the stable roof unit to the J edge of the previously pieced unit; add K to the top as shown in **Figure 4**. Press seams toward J and K.

Step 11. Sew L to opposite sides of the pieced unit; press seams toward L.

Step 12. Sew M to the top and bottom and N to opposite sides to complete the pieced top; press seams toward strips.

Adding Appliquéd Horses

Step 1. Prepare templates for horse head and neck/shoulder pieces using full-size patterns given. Cut as directed adding ¼" seam allowance when cutting for hand-appliqué. Turn under seam allowance all around each piece; baste to hold.

Step 2. Lay neck/shoulder pieces on A rectangles; pin in place. Place head pieces at different angles until you are satisfied with the arrangement of the pieces; pin them in place.

Step 3. Cut fringe into three 12" lengths. Tuck one length under the neck edge of one horse, bringing the top part of the fringe between the ears for the horse's forelock as shown in **Figure 5**; pin in place. Hand-appliqué the pieces in place. Repeat for each horse.

Step 4. Cut ¼"-wide red ribbon in three lengths each 3¾", 4" and 6½". Turn under ¼" on each end of ribbon strips; appliqué ribbon pieces on horses referring to the full-size pattern for placement.

Step 5. Trace three each eyes and nostrils on

LOG CABIN STABLE Placement Diagram 43" x 31½"

the paper side of the fusible web, reversing two of each before tracing. Fuse to wrong side of the brown mottled scrap.

Step 6. Cut out each shape on marked lines; remove paper backing. Fuse an eye and nostril shape on each head piece referring to the pattern for positioning.

Step 7. Hand-stitch mouth line using 3 strands dark brown embroidery floss and a stem stitch.

Step 8. Sew metal buttons to ribbon halters referring to the Placement Diagram for positioning. Sew ¾" wood-look buttons to J, spacing evenly across the strip.

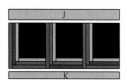

FIGURE 2 Join 3 Log Cabin blocks to make stable window unit; add J and K.

FIGURE 3 Join H triangles and add I to each end to make stable roof unit.

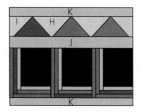

FIGURE 4 Join units as shown.

FIGURE 5 Place fringe under neck edge and bring top of fringe between ears for forelock.

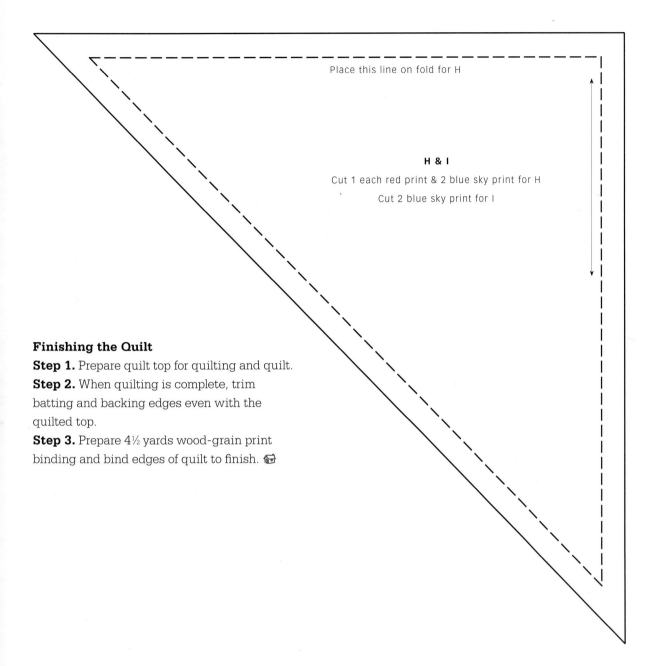

Place this line on fold for H

H & I

Cut 1 each red print & 2 blue sky print for H

Cut 2 blue sky print for I

Finishing the Quilt

Step 1. Prepare quilt top for quilting and quilt.

Step 2. When quilting is complete, trim batting and backing edges even with the quilted top.

Step 3. Prepare 4½ yards wood-grain print binding and bind edges of quilt to finish. 🏠

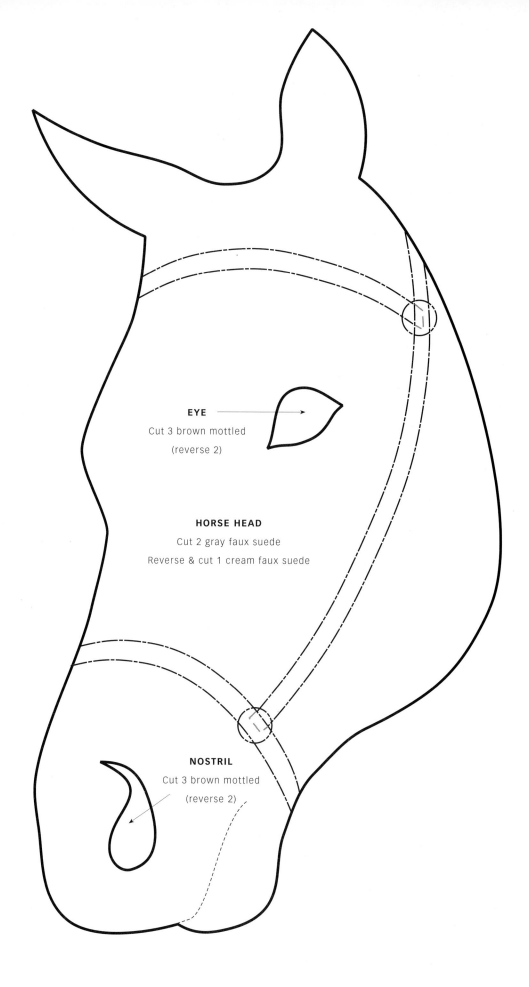

EYE
Cut 3 brown mottled
(reverse 2)

HORSE HEAD
Cut 2 gray faux suede
Reverse & cut 1 cream faux suede

NOSTRIL
Cut 3 brown mottled
(reverse 2)

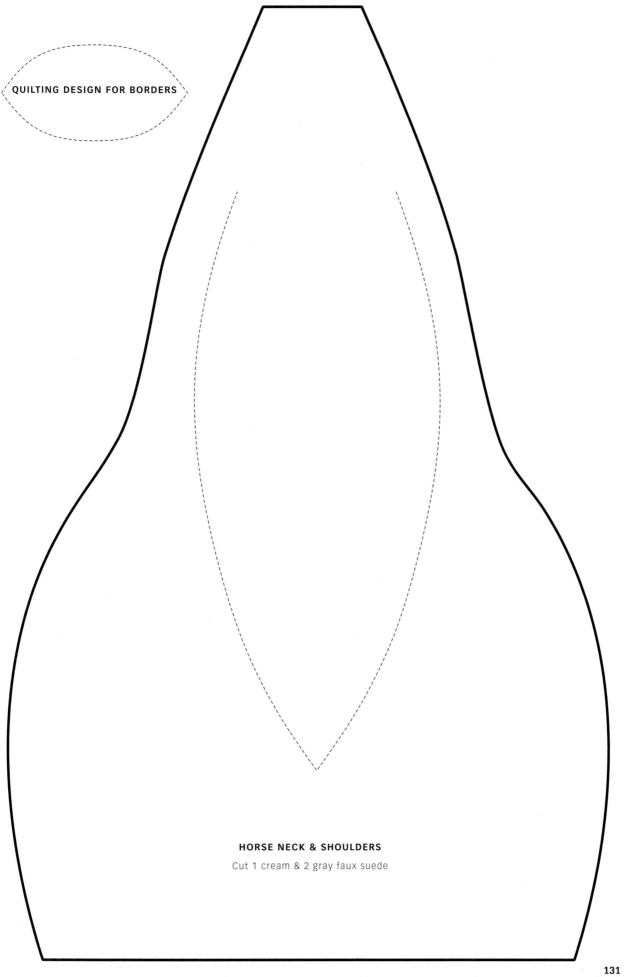

QUILTING DESIGN FOR BORDERS

HORSE NECK & SHOULDERS

Cut 1 cream & 2 gray faux suede

Whether on the bed or wall, today's Log Cabin quilts add the perfect finishing touch and bring a warm, welcoming look to any home.

DESIGN > RUTH SWASEY

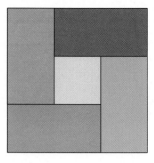

SIMPLIFIED LOG CABIN 1
6" X 6"

Simplified
Log Cabin

Lay out the pieces for the entire quilt before you stitch the blocks together, and you'll discover this quilt is very easy and quick to make.

PROJECT NOTE

The sample quilt uses many different batiks to form the patterned design. You may use as many as 30 different fabrics to make every pattern design different or fewer fabrics to add variety as in the project. Some fabrics are used once, while others are used three times.

PROJECT SPECIFICATIONS

Skill Level: Beginner

Quilt Size: 36" x 42"

Block Size: 6" x 6"

Number of Blocks: 42

MATERIALS

Note: All fabrics are batiks and will be referred to only by color in the list of materials and instructions.

- 6" x 10" rectangle 30 different fabrics
- ¼ yard yellow
- ⅓ yard multicolored for binding
- ½ yard navy blue
- Backing 42" x 48"
- Batting 42" x 48"
- Neutral color all-purpose thread
- Quilting thread
- Basic sewing tools and supplies

INSTRUCTIONS

Step 1. Cut three 2½" by fabric width strips yellow; subcut strips into 2½" square segments for A. You will need 42 A squares.

Step 2. Cut three strips 4½" by fabric width navy blue; subcut each strip into 2½" segments for B. You will 48 navy blue B pieces.

Step 3. Cut four 2½" x 4½" B rectangles from each 6" x 10" scrap.

Step 4. Before sewing begins, lay out pieces in blocks, and lay out blocks on a large flat surface. Four same-color B pieces form a design when four blocks meet as shown in **Figure 1**.

In order to create this design, every block is stitched in different color combinations with the yellow A center remaining the same. Outside-edge

FIGURE 1 The same-color B pieces form a design when 4 blocks meet.

blocks use two navy blue B pieces and corner blocks use three navy blue B pieces to create a border look referring to Figure 2.

Step 5. To piece one block, sew one B to A, stopping stitching 1" from the edge of A as shown in Figure 3. Press seam away from A.

Step 6. Add two more B pieces around A, starting on the complete-seam side as shown in Figure 4; press seams away from A. Add last B piece; complete unfinished beginning seam to complete one block as shown in Figure 5; press seam away from A.

Step 7. Piece 42 blocks keeping pieces in order arranged in Step 4, placing each block back in position after stitching to keep pattern organized.

Step 8. Join six blocks to make a row referring to Figure 6. Repeat for seven rows, placing each row in the arranged order after stitching. Press seams in alternating rows in opposite directions. Join rows to complete the pieced top.

Step 9. Prepare quilt top for quilting and quilt.

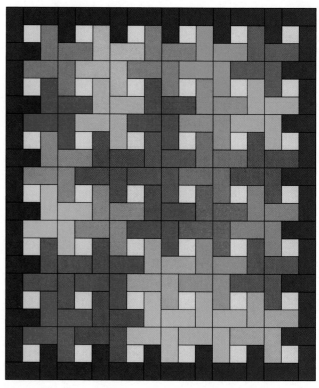

SIMPLIFIED LOG CABIN 1 Placement Diagram 36" x 42"

Step 10. When quilting is complete, trim batting and backing edges even with the quilted top.

Step 11. Prepare 5 yards mutlicolored binding and bind edges of quilt. 🏠

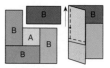

FIGURE 5 Add last B piece; complete unfinished seam to complete 1 block.

FIGURE 6 Join 6 blocks to make a row.

FIGURE 2 Create side and corner blocks with navy blue pieces.

FIGURE 3 Sew B to A, stopping stitching 1" from the edge of A.

FIGURE 4 Add 2 more B pieces around A, starting on the complete-seam side.

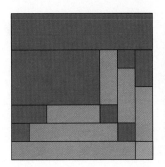

A BLOCK
10" x 10"

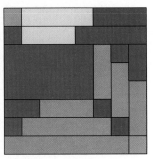

B BLOCK
10" x 10"

DESIGN > CHRISTINE SCHULTZ

C BLOCK
10" x 10"

Sylvan Flora

Flower centers are formed when pieced blocks converge in the right configuration.

PROJECT SPECIFICATIONS

Skill Level: Intermediate

Quilt Size: 68" x 88"

Block Size: 10" x 10"

Number of Blocks: 48

MATERIALS

Note: *All fabrics except green are batiks, mottleds or tone-on-tones and will be referred to by color in the list of materials and instructions.*

- ¼ yard each orange, teal, tangerine, yellow-orange, purple, lavender and blue
- ½ yard each yellow and pink
- ⅝ yard red
- 4½ yards green print
- Backing 74" x 94"
- Batting 74" x 94"
- Neutral color all-purpose thread
- Quilting thread
- Basic sewing tools and supplies

INSTRUCTIONS

Cutting

Step 1. From green print, cut two 3½" x 88½" Z strips and two 3½" x 62½" Y strips along the length of the fabric for border strips; set aside.

Step 2. From green print, cut seven 10½" x 10½" squares for D squares; set aside.

Step 3. From green print, cut 17 rectangles 3" x 10½" for A, 36 rectangles 4½" x 6¾" for B and five 8" x 9¼" rectangles for C.

Step 4. From green print, cut 22 strips 1¾" by fabric width; subcut seven strips into 1¾" square segments for D. You will need 163 D squares.

Step 5. From the remaining 1¾"-wide strips, cut the following: five 9¼" H, 24 each 4¼" G and 5½" F and seventy-two 3" E strips.

Step 6. Cut three strips 1¾" by fabric width orange; subcut into 1¾" square segments for DD. You will need 60 DD squares.

Step 7. Cut seven strips 1¾" by fabric width yellow; subcut into 24 each 4¼" GG pieces and 5½" FF pieces.

Step 8. Cut eight 1¾" by fabric width strips pink; subcut into thirty-two 4¼" KK and eight each 6¾" JJ and 9¼" HH strips.

Step 9. Cut four 1¾" by fabric width strips

each teal, blue, lavender, purple, tangerine, yellow-orange and red; subcut each color strip into sixteen 4¼" KK and four each 6¾" JJ and 9¼" HH strips.

Making A Blocks

Step 1. To make one pink A block, join green A, B, D and E pieces with orange DD and pink HH, JJ, KK pieces as shown in **Figure 1** to make strip units; press seams in one direction. Join the strip units to complete one pink A block; press seams in one direction.

Step 2. Repeat Step 1 to make A blocks in a variety of colors referring to **Figure 2** for placement of A blocks and colors needed. You will need three each teal and red, two each blue, purple and tangerine and five pink A blocks.

Making B Blocks

Step 1. To make one pink B block, join green B, D, E, F and G pieces with orange DD, yellow GG and FF, and pink HH, JJ and KK pieces as shown in **Figure 3** to make strip units; press seams in one direction. Join strip units to complete one pink B block; press seams in one direction.

Step 2. Repeat Step 1 to make B blocks in a variety of colors referring to **Figure 2** for placement of B blocks and colors needed. You will need one each red and teal, two each tangerine, blue and purple, three pink, and four each lavender and yellow-orange B blocks.

Making C Blocks

Step 1. To make one C block, join green C, G, F and H pieces with orange DD and yellow FF and GG pieces as shown in **Figure 4** to make strip units; press seams in one direction. Join strip units to complete one C block; press seams in one direction. Repeat for five C blocks.

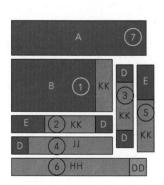

FIGURE 1 Join cut pieces to make pieced units; join the units to complete an A block.

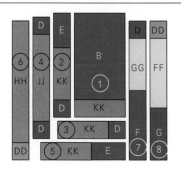

FIGURE 3 Join cut pieces to make pieced units; join the units to complete a B block.

D	D	D	D	A pink	A pink
D	C	C	C	B pink	A pink
D	C	B lavender	B lavender	B tangerine	A tangerine
D	C	B lavender	B lavender	B tangerine	A tangerine
A pink	B pink	B yellow-orange	B yellow-orange	B blue	A blue
A pink	B pink	B yellow-orange	B yellow-orange	B blue	A blue
A teal	B teal	B purple	B purple	B red	A red
A teal	A teal	A purple	A purple	A red	A red

FIGURE 2 Letters refer to pieced blocks and colors refer to the color of each block.

Completing the Top

Step 1. Arrange the pieced blocks with green print D squares in eight rows of six blocks each referring to **Figure 2** and the Placement Diagram for block and color placement.

Step 2. Join the blocks in rows as arranged; press seams in alternating rows in opposite directions. Join the rows to complete the pieced center; press seams in one direction.

Step 3. Cut and piece two 1½" x 60½" W strips and two 1½" x 82½" X strips red. Sew a W strip to the top and bottom and an X strip to opposite long sides of the pieced center; press seams toward strips.

Step 4. Sew a previously cut Y strip to the top and bottom and the previously cut Z strips to opposite sides of the pieced center; press seams toward strips.

Finishing the Quilt

Step 1. Prepare quilt top for quilting and quilt. **Note:** *The sample quilt was hand-quilted in the colored sections of the blocks using the patterns given and cream hand-quilting thread as shown in* **Figures 5–7**. *The large green print sections were randomly quilted with the designs given.*

Step 2. When quilting is complete, trim batting and backing edges even with the quilted top.

Step 3. Prepare 9¼ yards green print binding and bind edges of quilt to finish. 🏠

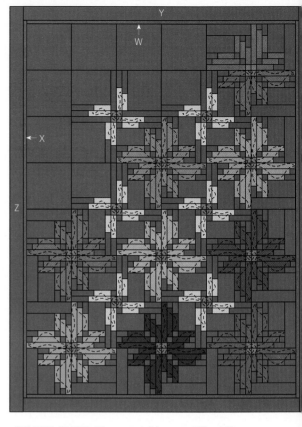

SYLVAN FLORA Placement Diagram 68" x 88"

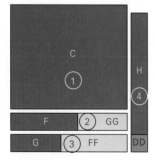

FIGURE 4 Join cut pieces to make pieced units; join the units to complete a C block.

FIGURE 5 The quilting designs given were quilted in the B block sections as shown.

FIGURE 6 The quilting designs given were quilted in the A block sections as shown.

FIGURE 7 The quilting designs given were quilted in the C block sections as shown.

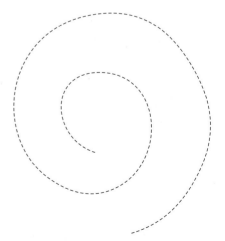

QUILTING DESIGN FOR DD SQUARE SECTIONS

QUILTING DESIGN FOR SMALL
COLORED SECTIONS

QUILTING
DESIGN FOR
YELLOW
SECTIONS

QUILTING DESIGN FOR LARGE COLORED
SECTIONS

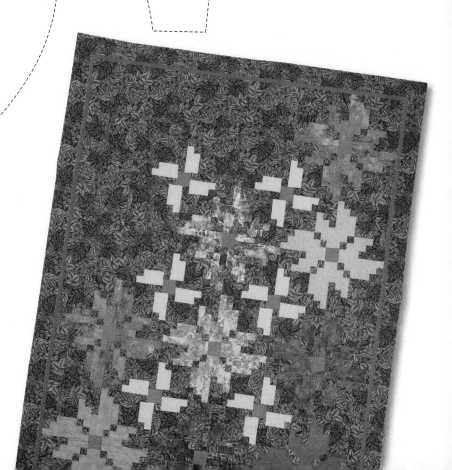

TULIPS AROUND THE CABIN

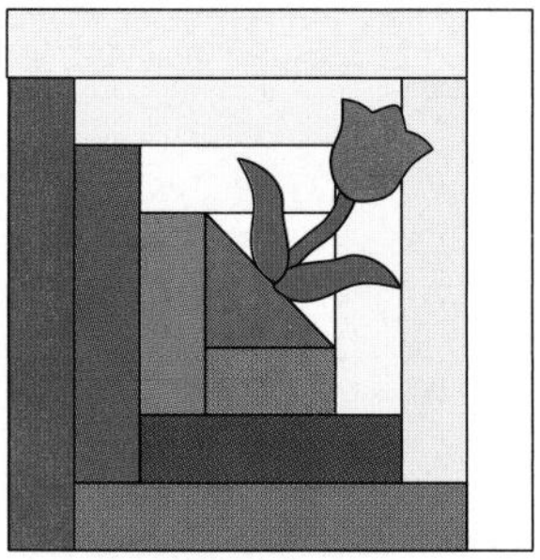

12" x 12" Block

Tulips Around the Cabin

Gather up your light and dark scraps to make this combination pieced-and-appliquéd quilt.

PROJECT SPECIFICATIONS

Skill Level: Beginner

Quilt Size: 88½" x 88½"

Block Size: 12" x 12"

Number of Blocks: 36

MATERIALS

- ⅛ yard each yellow, red, blue and purple mottleds for flowers
- ¼ yard dark green print for stems and leaves
- 1 yard white print for block centers and sashing
- 1 yard burgundy print for outside border
- 2 yards black print for block centers, sashing, border and binding
- 3 yards total each light and dark scraps for block piecing
- Backing 95" x 95"
- Batting 95" x 95"
- Neutral color and black all-purpose thread
- Quilting thread
- 1¼ yards fusible web
- 1⅔ yards fabric stabilizer
- Basic sewing tools and supplies

INSTRUCTIONS

Making Log Cabin Blocks

Step 1. Cut 18 squares each white and black prints 3⅞" x 3⅞" for A. Draw a line from corner to corner on the wrong side of the white print A squares.

Step 2. Place a white print A on a black print A with right sides together; stitch ¼" on each side of the marked line as shown in **Figure 1**. Cut apart on the marked line and press open to make two A units as shown in **Figure 2**; repeat for 36 A units.

Step 3. Cut the light and dark scraps into 2"-wide strips; cut into 36 pieces of each of the following lengths: light strips—5", 6½", 8", 9½", 11", and 12½"; dark strips—3½", 5", 6½", 8", 9½" and 11".

Step 4. Sew the shortest dark strip to the dark

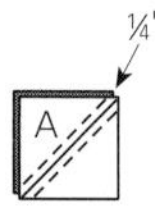

FIGURE 1 Stitch ¼" on each side of line.

FIGURE 2 Cut apart on line to make 2 A units.

print side of an A unit; press the shortest dark strip; press seam toward strip. Continue to add strips to the sides of the center as shown in **Figure 3**. Press all seams toward the most recently added strip. Complete 36 blocks.

Step 5. Trace appliqué shapes onto the paper side of the fusible web as directed on the pieces for number to cut. Cut out shapes leaving a margin around each one.

Step 6. Fuse shapes to the wrong side of the fabrics as directed on pieces for color; cut out shapes on the traced lines. Remove paper backing.

Step 7. Arrange one flower, one stem, and one leaf and reversed leaf on the light side of a completed Log Cabin block referring to the block drawing for positioning; fuse shapes in place. Repeat for all blocks.

Step 8. Cut 36 rectangles fabric stabilizer 5" x 6"; pin behind each fused shape.

Step 9. Using black all-purpose thread, buttonhole-stitch around each shape. When stitching is complete, remove fabric stabilizer.

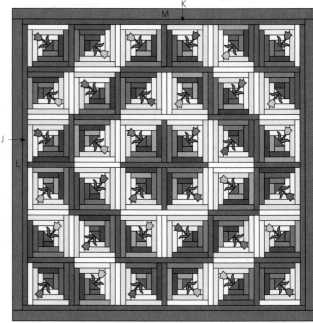

TULIPS AROUND THE CABIN Placement Diagram 88½" x 88½"

Completing the Top

Step 1. Cut and piece two 2" x 80" J strips and two 2" x 83" K strips black print; set aside for borders. Cut nine 2¼" by fabric width strips black print; set aside for binding.

Step 2. Cut the remaining white and black prints into 2" by fabric width strips for sashing strips. Subcut the white print strips into

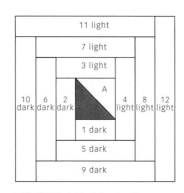

FIGURE 3 Add strips to the sides of the center A unit.

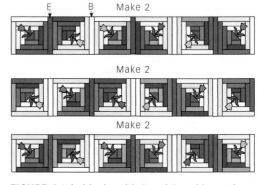

FIGURE 4 Join blocks with B and E sashing strips.

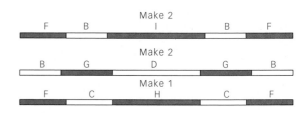

FIGURE 5 Join sashing strips to make sashing rows.

twenty-two 12½" B, two 14" C and two 26" D sashing strips. Subcut the black print strips into sixteen 12½" E, six 14" F, four 15½" G, one 26" H and two 29" I sashing strips.

Step 3. Join six blocks with B and E sashing strips to make a block row as shown in **Figure 4**; press seams toward sashing strips. Repeat for six block rows.

Step 4. Join remaining sashing strips to make sashing rows as shown in **Figure 5**; press seams toward white print strips.

Step 5. Join the block rows and sashing rows to complete the pieced center as shown in Figure 6; press seams toward sashing rows.

Step 6. Sew J strips to opposite sides and K strips to the top and bottom of the pieced center; press seams toward J and K.

Step 7. Cut and piece two 3½" x 83" L strips and two 3½" x 89" M strips burgundy print. Sew L strips to opposite sides and M strips to the top and bottom of the pieced center; press seams toward L and M.

Finishing the Quilt

Step 1. Prepare quilt top for quilting and quilt.

Step 2. When quilting is complete, trim batting and backing edges even with the quilted top.

Step 3. Prepare 10⅜ yards black print binding using previously cut strips and bind edges of quilt to finish. 🏠

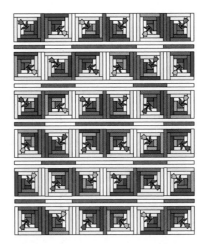

FIGURE 6 Join block rows and sashing rows to complete the pieced center.

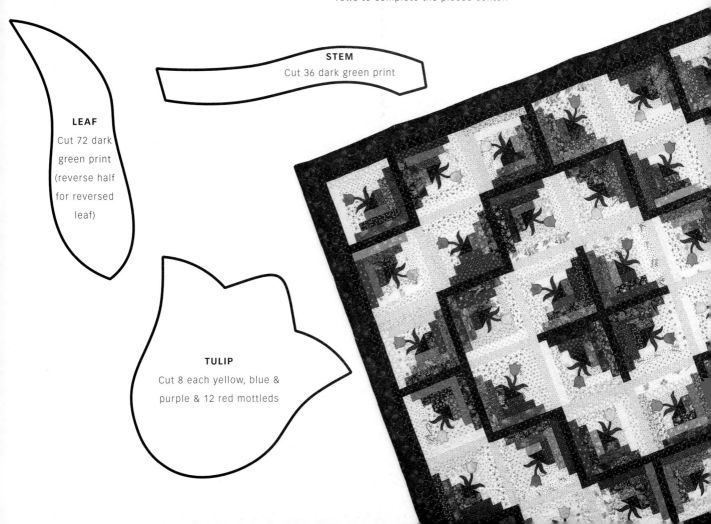

STEM
Cut 36 dark green print

LEAF
Cut 72 dark green print (reverse half for reversed leaf)

TULIP
Cut 8 each yellow, blue & purple & 12 red mottleds

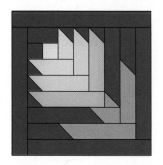

TULIP
9" x 9" Block

Tulip
Quartet

Pieced tulip blocks combine both foundation piecing and quick angle piecing to make the fabric flowers.

PROJECT SPECIFICATIONS

Skill Level: Intermediate

Quilt Size: 22" x 22"

Block Size: 9" x 9"

Number of Blocks: 4

MATERIALS

- 1 square each yellow and navy solids, and 2 squares white solid 1½" x 1½" for piece 1
- 1½"-wide scrap strips green, lavender, blue, yellow and orange prints, solids, mottleds or tone-on-tones
- ¼ yard green print for binding
- ²⁄₄ yard dark blue print
- Backing 28" x 28"
- Batting 28" x 28"
- Neutral color all-purpose thread
- Quilting thread
- 3 (1") plastic rings
- Basic sewing tools and supplies

INSTRUCTIONS

Step 1. Prepare four copies of the foundation pattern given.

Step 2. Cut seven strips 1½" by fabric width dark blue print for BG strips.

Step 3. To piece one yellow block, begin with the yellow solid piece 1 and add pieces 2 and 3 referring to pattern for color and to pages 6–8 for instructions.

Step 4. To make odd-numbered background triangle ends as in pieces 4 and 5, cut six 1½" square segments from the BG strips; mark a diagonal line on the wrong side of each square. Pin a square right sides together on one end of a yellow strip as shown in **Figure 1**; stitch on the diagonal of the BG square, again referring to **Figure 1**.

Step 5. Trim seam to ¼"; press BG to the right side as shown in **Figure 2**. Pin the

FIGURE 1 Pin a BG square to a yellow strip; stitch on the diagonal of the BG square.

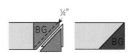

FIGURE 2 Trim seam to ¼"; press BG to the right side.

147

stitched unit to the stitched foundation in the 4/5 position, matching edge of BG with outside line of foundation and positioning unit ¼" inside the 4/5 seam line as shown in **Figure 3**. Stitch and trim excess yellow strip as for pieces 1–3.

Step 6. Continue adding BG squares to yellow strips and stitching to the foundation. Complete the pieced section with a BG strip and a 1½" x 1½" square green.

Step 7. To make remaining units for one block, cut one piece each from green strips as follows: 2½" for piece 18, 3½" for piece 19 and 4½" for piece 20. Cut pieces from BG strips as follows: two each 4½" (pieces 19 and 20) and 8½" (pieces 22 and 23) and one each 5½" (piece 18), 7½" (piece 21) and 9½" (piece 24). **Note:** *Cut all green strips for one block from the same green scrap.*

Step 8. To piece unit 18, place the 1½" x 2½" green piece on the 1½" x 5½" BG piece, stitch and trim to complete unit 18 as in Steps 4 and 5, and as shown in **Figure 4**.

Step 9. Add unit 18 to the pieced unit referring to **Figure 5**; press seams toward unit 18.

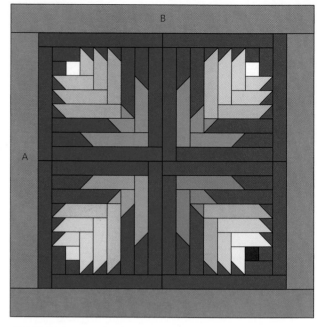

TULIP QUARTET Placement Diagram 22" x 22"

Step 10. Continue piecing BG and green pieces to complete units 19 and 20 referring to **Figure 6** for strip angle. Add to the pieced unit, referring to Figure 7 for positioning of pieces.

Step 11. Add BG pieces 21–24, again referring to **Figure 7** for positioning of pieces.

Step 12. Repeat for one block each in lavender (with white solid piece 1), blue (with navy

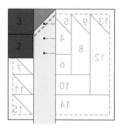

FIGURE 3 Pin the stitched unit to the stitched foundation in the 4/5 position, matching edge of BG with outside line of foundation.

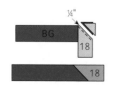

FIGURE 4 Complete unit 18.

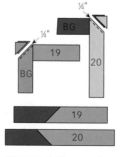

FIGURE 5 Add unit 18 to the pieced unit.

FIGURE 6 Piece units 19 and 20 as shown.

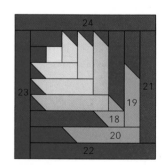

FIGURE 7 Add the remaining units and BG strips to complete 1 block.

solid piece 1) and orange (with white solid piece 1).

Step 13. Join two blocks to make a row referring to the Placement Diagram for positioning of blocks; press seams in one direction. Repeat for second row; press seams in opposite direction. Join the rows to complete the pieced center.

Step 14. Cut two 2½" x 18½" A and two 2½" x 22½" B strips dark blue print. Sew A to opposite sides and B to the top and bottom of the pieced center; press seams toward strips.

Note: *The designer used the wrong side of the dark blue print as the right side of the A and B strips on the sample.*

Step 15. Prepare quilt top for quilting and quilt.

Step 16. When quilting is complete, trim batting and backing edges even with the quilted top.

Step 17. Prepare 3 yards green print binding and bind edges of quilt.

Step 18. Sew a plastic ring at each top corner and at center edge on back of quilt to hang. 🏠

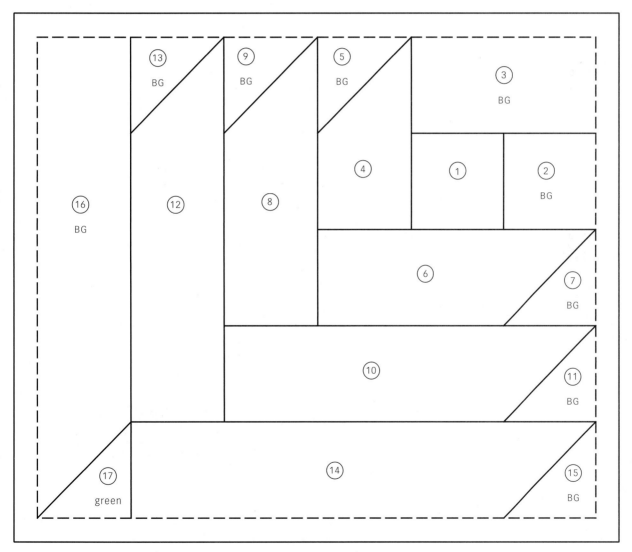

FOUNDATION PATTERN
Make 4 copies

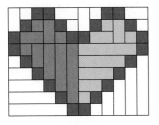

LOG CABIN HEART

18" x 13½" Block

Joined
Hearts

Many different strip set combinations create the block units in this patterned Log Cabin design.

PROJECT SPECIFICATIONS

Skill Level: Intermediate

Quilt Size: 69" x 82½"

Block Size: 18" x 13½"

Number of Blocks: 15

MATERIALS

- 1⅛ yards pink print
- 2 yards white print
- 2⅛ yards burgundy mottled
- 2⅜ yards red print
- Backing 75" x 88"
- Batting 75" x 88"
- Neutral color all-purpose thread
- Quilting thread
- Basic sewing tools and supplies

INSTRUCTIONS

Preparing Segments for Piecing

Step 1. Cut the following 2" by fabric width strips: three each red and pink prints, five white print and 23 burgundy mottled.

Step 2. Join the strips with right sides together along length to make three strip sets each burgundy/red A and burgundy/pink K, and five burgundy/white B; press seams toward darker fabric.

Step 3. Subcut strip sets into 2" segments to make 45 each A and K segments, and 90 B segments as shown in **Figure 1**.

Step 4. Cut the following 3½" by fabric width strips: three each red and pink prints, and five white print.

Step 5. Join 2" burgundy mottled strips with red and pink print strips as in Step 2 to make three strip sets each burgundy/pink L and burgundy/red D; press seams toward darker fabric.

Step 6. Subcut the white print strips into ninety 2" segments for C and the strip sets into 2" segments to make 45 each L and D segments as shown in **Figure 2**.

Step 7. Cut one strip each red and pink prints and two strips white print 5" by fabric width. Join 2" burgundy mottled strips

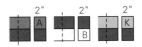

FIGURE 1 Subcut strip sets into 2" segments to make A, B and K segments.

with red and pink print strips as in Step 2 to make the following strip sets: one each burgundy/pink M and burgundy/red F.

Step 8. Subcut the white print strips into thirty 2" segments for E and the strip sets into 2" segments to make 15 each F and M segments as shown in **Figure 3**.

Step 9. Cut one strip each red and pink prints and two strips white print 6½" by fabric width. Join 2" burgundy mottled strips with red and pink print strips as in Step 2 to make one strip set each burgundy/pink N and burgundy/red H.

Step 10. Subcut the white print strips into thirty 2" segments for G and the strip sets into 2" segments to make 15 each H and N segments as shown in **Figure 4**.

Step 11. Cut one strip each red and pink prints and two strips white print 8" by fabric width. Join 2" burgundy mottled strips with red and pink print strips as in Step 2 to make one strip set each burgundy/pink O and burgundy/red J.

Step 12. Subcut the white print strips into thirty 2" segments for I and the strip sets into

JOINED HEARTS Placement Diagram 69" x 82½"

2" segments to make 15 each J and O segments as shown in **Figure 5**.

Piecing the Blocks

Step 1. To make one Log Cabin Heart block, join an A and B segment and add C and D as shown in **Figure 6**. Repeat for two units and

FIGURE 2 Subcut the strip sets into 2" segments to make D and L segments.

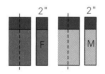

FIGURE 3 Subcut the strip sets into 2" segments to make F and M segments.

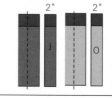

FIGURE 4 Subcut strip sets into 2" segments to make H and N segments.

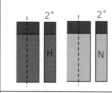

FIGURE 5 Subcut strip sets into 2" segments to make J and O segments.

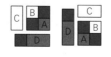

FIGURE 6 Join an A and B segment and add C and D.

FIGURE 7 Join pieced units as shown.

FIGURE 8 Join a B and K segment and add C and L.

join as shown in **Figure 7**. Press all seams toward most recently added strip or segment.

Step 2. Join B and K segments and add C and L referring to **Figure 8**; repeat for two units. Join units as shown in **Figure 9**. Press all seams toward most recently added strip or segment.

Step 3. Join the two pieced units to complete the top part of the block as shown in **Figure 10**. Press seam in one direction.

Step 4. Join A and B segments and add C and D as in Step 1; continue to add remaining white print E, G and I pieces with F, H and J segments referring to **Figure 11** to complete one Log Cabin unit for bottom half of the block. Press all seams toward the most recently added strip or segment.

Step 5. Join B and K segments and add C and L as in Step 2; continue to add remaining white print E, G and I pieces with M, N and O segments referring to **Figure 12** to complete a second Log Cabin unit for bottom half of the block. Press all seams toward the most recently added strip or segment.

Step 6. Join the two Log Cabin units to complete the bottom half of the block as shown in **Figure 13**; press seam in opposite direction from top half of block.

Step 7. Join the two pieced block sections to complete one Heart block as shown in **Figure 14**; repeat for 15 blocks. Press seams in one direction.

Completing the Top

Step 1. Arrange the pieced blocks in five rows of three blocks each referring to the Placement Diagram.

Step 2. Join blocks in rows; press seams in adjacent rows in opposite directions.

Step 3. Join rows to complete the pieced top; press seams in one direction.

Step 4. Cut and piece two 2" x 68" P strips and two 2" x 57½" Q strips burgundy mottled. Sew P to opposite long sides and Q to the top and bottom of the pieced center; press seams toward P and Q.

Step 5. Cut and piece two 6½" x 71" R strips and two 6½" x 69½" S strips red print. Sew R to opposite long sides and S to the top and bottom of the pieced center; press seams toward R and S.

Finishing the Quilt

Step 1. Prepare quilt top for quilting and quilt.

Step 2. When quilting is complete, trim batting and backing edges even with the quilted top.

Step 3. Prepare 9 yards burgundy mottled binding and bind edges of quilt to finish. 🏠

FIGURE 9 Join pieced units as shown.

FIGURE 11 Join segments and pieces to complete a Log Cabin unit.

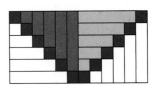

FIGURE 13 Join the 2 Log Cabin units to complete the bottom half of the block.

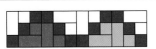

FIGURE 10 Join the 2 pieced units to complete the top part of the block.

FIGURE 12 Join segments and pieces to complete a Log Cabin unit.

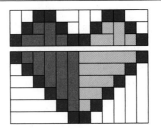

FIGURE 14 Join the 2 pieced block sections to complete 1 Heart block.

DESIGN > CYNTHIA MYERBERG

RULES OF CHAOS #8
Approximately 7" x 7" Block

Rules of
Chaos

The Rules of Chaos series is influenced by the vibrant colors and simple, stark geometry of traditional and antique Amish quilts.

PROJECT NOTES

Traditional quiltmaking requires strict adherence to measurements, methods of construction and use of templates. I choose to bend the rules. Free-form cutting and an improvisational approach to design give the resulting quilts a more fluid, organic look than their predecessors. Geometric forms are mixed, skewed and stretched. I hand-dye all of the 100-percent cotton fabrics that make up the quilts. I strive for uneven hues that simulate the patina of the antique quilts by folding and crumpling the fabric in the dye bath, often achieving a suede-like surface. Contemporary quiltmaking tools and ideas bring these quilts to the 21st century. Assembly and quilting are done by machine.

For freehand-cutting Rules of Chaos quilts, the shapes and strips are cut slightly larger than for a conventional quilt because you need to overlap each piece and cut it to fit.

Rules of Chaos #8
PROJECT SPECIFICATIONS

Skill Level: Advanced

Quilt Size: Approximately 21" x 56"

Block Size: Approximately 7" x 7"

Number of Blocks: 24

MATERIALS

- Scraps of a variety of hand-dyed fabrics in light and dark values
- ¾ yards black solid
- Backing 27" x 62"
- Batting 27" x 62"
- Neutral color all-purpose thread
- Quilting thread
- Basic sewing tools and supplies

INSTRUCTIONS
Piecing Free-Form Blocks
Step 1. Use a rotary cutter to freehand-cut a

rectangle approximately 4½" x 3" for A. Do not try to make it a perfect rectangle, but give it a slightly lopsided shape as shown in **Figure 1**. **Note:** *If your rectangle is considerably smaller than the recommended size, make the surrounding strips wider to make up the difference. A variety in the size of the rectangles and strips gives this quilt a more contemporary look.*

Step 2. Freehand-cut a contrasting fabric in strips approximately 1¾"–2¼" wide for B and C. Label the narrower strips B and the wider strips C.

Step 3. Lay the long edge of A next to a B strip and cut B at least ½" longer than A. Overlap the edges of A and B slightly as shown in **Figure 2**.

Step 4. Using the edge of A as a guide, cut the strip along the edge of A following the shape suggested by A as shown in **Figure 3**. **Note:** *Do not square off these strips, but rather, follow the shape of the block.* Sew B to A; press seam to one side. Trim B ends even with A.

Step 5. Lay the top edge of the A-B unit next to a C strip. Slightly overlap the edges. Using the edge of the A-B unit as a guide, cut the C strip along the edge of A-B as shown in **Figure 4**. Trim off ends to follow the shape of the block and sew C to the A-B unit; press seams to one side.

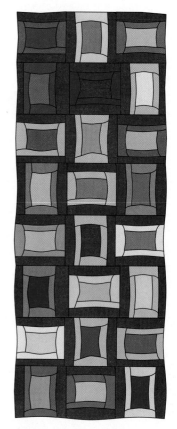

RULES OF CHAOS #8
Placement Diagram 21" x 56"

Step 6. Continue to build the block in this manner until you have surrounded the center A with the contrasting fabric using wider C strips for the top and bottom of the rectangle and narrower B strips for the sides as shown in **Figure 5**.

Step 7. Freehand-cut black solid strips

FIGURE 1 A should be slightly lopsided.

FIGURE 2 Overlap the edges of A and B slightly.

FIGURE 3 Cut the B strip along the edge of A following the shape suggested by A.

FIGURE 4 Using the edge of the A-B unit as a guide, cut the C strip along the edge of A-B.

FIGURE 5 Use wider strips for the top and bottom of the rectangle and narrower strips for the sides.

approximately 2¼" wide. Cut two strips that are at least ½" longer than the sides of the pieced unit. Lay the long edge of the pieced unit next to a black strip, slightly overlapping the strip. Using the edge of the rectangle as a guide, cut the strip along the edge of the rectangle. Sew on the black strip.

Step 8. Repeat this process on the other side of the pieced unit as shown in **Figure 6**; press seam to one side. Trim off ends to follow the shape of the block.

Step 9. Measure the block; it should be a rectangular shape. Don't worry about the exact size and don't trim anything until you are ready to assemble the quilt.

Step 10. Repeat the process to make 24 blocks that are close to the same size.

Completing the Top

Step 1. Arrange the pieced blocks on a design wall until the color placement is pleasing.

Step 2. Lay out the first row of three blocks on your cutting surface referring to **Figure 7**, lining up according to size. **Note:** *If all three blocks are approximately the same size, you have been lucky.* Overlap one block over the black strip of the second block and cut using the top block as a guide.

Step 3. Sew the two blocks together; press seams in one direction. **Note:** *If one block is longer/shorter than the other, leave it for now. Don't trim off excess until you are ready to join the rows.*

Step 4. Place row 2 on the cutting surface; line up blocks as shown in **Figure 8**. Overlap, cut, sew and press as in Steps 2 and 3. Repeat for all rows.

Step 5. Lay rows 1 and 2 on the cutting surface. Line up the rows, centering the center blocks. **Note:** *Don't worry if seams don't meet.* Freehand-trim the bottom edge of the top row as shown in **Figure 9**, remembering that these should not be too straight, but slightly curved. Sew row 1 to row 2; press seam to one side.

Step 6. Continue sewing one row to the next in the same manner until the top is complete; press seams in one direction.

Step 7. When the top is complete, freehand-trim around the entire piece, trimming all uneven edges.

Finishing the Quilt

Step 1. Prepare quilt top for quilting and quilt.

Step 2. When quilting is complete, trim batting and backing edges even with the quilted top.

Step 3. Prepare 4¾ yards black solid bias binding and bind edges of quilt to finish.

Note: *The binding should be made of bias*

FIGURE 6 Repeat this process on the other side of the pieced unit.

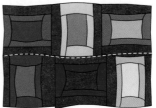

FIGURE 8 Place row 2 on the cutting surface; line up blocks.

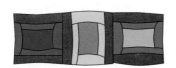

FIGURE 7 Lay out the first row of 3 blocks.

FIGURE 9 Freehand-trim the bottom edge of the top row.

strips because the edges of the quilt are not perfectly straight and require some curved stitching.

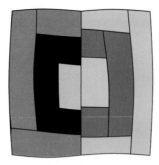

RULES OF CHAOS #9

Approximately 8" x 8" Block

Rules of Chaos #9

This quilt is made using the same methods as Rules of Chaos #8 except that the blocks are almost square before they are cut in half and rearranged to create a whole new look.

PROJECT SPECIFICATIONS

Skill Level: Advanced

Quilt Size: 28" x 44"

Block Size: Approximately 8" x 8"

Number of Blocks: 15

RULES OF CHAOS #9 Placement Diagram 28" x 44"

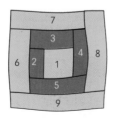

FIGURE 10 Sew strips around the center in the order shown.

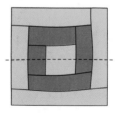

FIGURE 11 Freehand-cut each block in half.

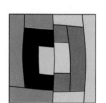

FIGURE 13 Join 2 half-blocks to make a block.

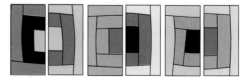

FIGURE 12 Pair the cut half-blocks and arrange in a row.

MATERIALS

- Scraps of a variety of hand-dyed fabrics in light and dark values
- 1¼ yards black solid
- Backing 34" x 50"
- Batting 34" x 50"
- Neutral color all-purpose thread
- Quilting thread
- Basic sewing tools and supplies

INSTRUCTIONS

Making Blocks

Step 1. Freehand-cut strips of light and dark fabrics and black solid 1½", 1¾", 2", 2¼" and 2½" wide.

Step 2. Freehand-cut squares that are approximately 2½", 3½" and 4" square. **Note:** *Use a variety of sizes of squares and strips to create visual interest.*

Step 3. Begin with any square and a different color strip; sew the strip to the square referring to page 154 for instructions. Continue to add strips around the square referring to **Figure 10** for order of piecing and to pages 9–11 for instructions. **Note:** *For consistent-size blocks, use the following formula: 4" square with 1½" and 2¼" strips; 3½" square with 1¾" and 2¼" strips; 2½" square with 2" and 2½" strips.*

Step 4. Measure the finished block and trim to 9" x 9". Repeat to make 15 blocks.

Completing the Top

Step 1. Freehand-cut each block in half as shown in **Figure 11**.

Step 2. Pair the cut half-blocks and arrange in five rows of three pair each referring to **Figure 12** for one row. Move block halves around until you are satisfied with the arrangement.

Step 3. Join half-blocks to make squares as shown in **Figure 13**; trim blocks to 8½" x 8½" to make square again after stitching, keeping center seam centered.

Step 4. Lay the blocks out in rows again and join to make a row; repeat for five rows. Press seams in adjacent rows in opposite directions. Join the rows to complete the pieced center; press seams in one direction.

Step 5. Cut two 2½" x 40½" A strips and two 2½" x 28½" B strips black solid. Sew A to opposite long sides and B to the top and bottom of the pieced center; press seams toward strips.

Finishing the Quilt

Step 1. Finish as for Rules of Chaos #8 except make 4½ yards black bias binding. 🏠

DESIGN > JULIE WEAVER

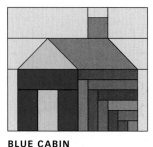

BLUE CABIN
14" x 12" Block

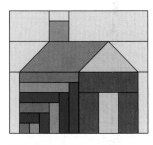

RED CABIN
14" x 12" Block

Patriotic
Cabins

Frame the center Cabin blocks with
a pieced-block border to make a
pretty Log Cabin wall quilt.

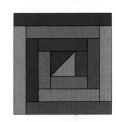

SMALL LOG CABIN
4" x 4" Block

PROJECT SPECIFICATIONS

Skill Level: Intermediate

Quilt Size: 24" x 48"

Block Size: 4" x 4" and 14" x 12"

Number of Blocks: 32 and 3

MATERIALS

- ⅛ yard cream print for doors and peaks
- ¼ yard each 4 different blue prints
- ¼ yard each 4 different red prints
- ¼ yard blue tone-on-tone for roofs
- ¼ yard red tone-on-tone for roof
- ⅓ yard red/blue print for binding
- ½ yard tan tone-on-tone for background
- 1¼ yards muslin for foundation piecing
- Backing 30" x 54"
- Batting 30" x 54"
- Neutral color all-purpose thread
- Quilting thread
- Basic sewing tools and supplies

INSTRUCTIONS

Making Red and Blue Cabin Blocks

Step 1. Cut one 1½" by fabric width strip from

each of the four red prints.

Step 2. Cut one 8" x 8" square muslin.

Step 3. Cut one 1½" x 1½" square from two
different strips for pieces 1 and 2. Begin approximately 1" from the lower right corner of
the muslin foundation by placing piece 1 right
side up on the muslin.

Step 4. Place piece 2 right sides together
with piece 1 and stitch referring to **Figure 1**;
press open.

Step 5. Cut a 1½" x 2½" piece from one strip
for piece 3; place piece 3 right sides together
with stitched 1-2 and stitch as shown in
Figure 2. Press open.

FIGURE 1 Place piece 2
right sides together with
piece 1 and stitch.

FIGURE 2 Place piece
3 right sides together
with stitched 1-2 and
stitch.

Step 6. Referring to **Figure 3** for sizes and order of piecing, cut red strips and stitch in place to complete one red cabin unit. Repeat for two red cabin units.

Step 7. Repeat Steps 1–5 with blue print fabrics and reversed pattern as shown in **Figure 4** to complete one blue cabin unit.

Step 8. Measure and square cabin units to 6½" x 6½".

Step 9. Referring to **Figure 5** for sizes to cut and order of piecing, cut fabric pieces for Red and Blue Cabin blocks as directed.

Step 10. For one Blue Cabin block, join pieces 1, 2 and 3, and add 4 and then 5 to piece door unit as shown in **Figure 6**; press seams as you stitch.

Step 11. Sew the 1–5 unit to a red cabin unit and add piece 12 as shown in **Figure 7**; press seams away from the cabin unit.

Step 12. To make a blue roof section, place piece 2 on the left end of piece 1; draw a diagonal line as shown in **Figure 8**. Stitch on the marked line; trim seam to ¼" and press open as shown in **Figure 9**.

Step 13. Place piece 3 on the right end of the pieced unit; mark, stitch, trim and press as in Step 12 and referring to **Figure 10**. Repeat with piece 4 referring to **Figure 11**, to complete a blue roof section.

Step 14. Sew the roof section to the top of the pieced cabin section as shown in **Figure 12**; press seam toward the roof section.

Step 15. To piece the chimney section, sew piece 2 to piece 1, and add pieces 3 and 4 as shown in **Figure 13**; press seams away from pieces 1 and 2.

Step 16. Sew the chimney section to the top of the pieced roof/cabin unit to complete one Blue Cabin block as shown in **Figure 14**; repeat for two blocks.

Step 17. Piece one Red Cabin block as in Steps 10–16 using red tone-on-tone and the blue cabin unit, and referring to **Figure 15**.

Making Small Log Cabin Blocks

Step 1. Cut five 1⅞" x 1⅞" squares from each of the four different red and blue prints for small block centers; set aside eight red and eight blue squares for another use.

Step 2. Place a red and blue square right sides together; draw a diagonal line from corner to corner on the wrong side of one of the squares. Stitch on the marked line; trim ¼" from stitched line and press open to make triangle/square block centers referring to **Figure 16**. Repeat for 32 triangle/squares.

Step 3. Cut 32 muslin squares 6" x 6" for foundations.

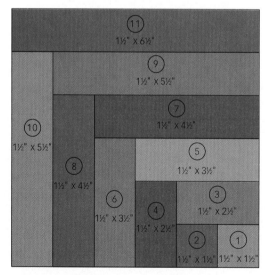

FIGURE 3 Cut red strips and stitch in place to complete 1 red cabin unit.

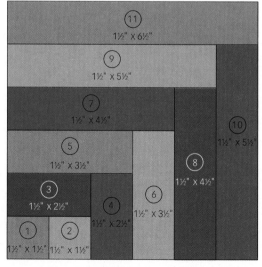

FIGURE 4 Cut blue strips, reverse pattern and stitch in place to complete 1 blue cabin unit.

Step 4. Cut several 1" by fabric width strips from each of the red and blue prints.

Step 5. Place a triangle/square right side up on the center of one muslin square with red half pointing toward the upper left corner as shown in **Figure 17**.

Step 6. Referring to **Figure 18**, cut pieces in sizes and colors as marked; stitch to center triangle/square unit in numerical order,

pressing each strip to the right side after stitching, to complete one Small Log Cabin block. Repeat for 32 blocks.

Step 7. When all blocks are complete, trim to 4½" x 4½".

Completing the Top

Step 1. Cut two 1½" x 14½" X strips tan-on-tan print. Join the two Blue Cabin blocks with

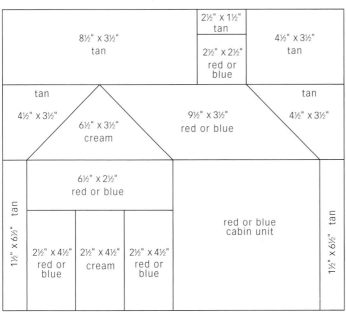

FIGURE 5 Cut fabric pieces for Red and Blue Cabin blocks as marked for size and color.

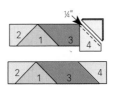

FIGURE 11 Add piece 4 to complete a blue roof section.

FIGURE 12 Sew the roof section to the top of the pieced cabin section.

FIGURE 13 Complete a chimney section as shown.

FIGURE 6 Join pieces 1, 2 and 3 and add 4 and then 5 to make a door unit.

FIGURE 7 Sew the 1–5 unit and piece 12 to a red cabin unit.

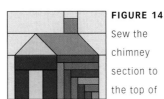

FIGURE 14 Sew the chimney section to the top of the pieced roof/cabin unit to complete 1 Blue Cabin block.

FIGURE 8 Place piece 2 on the left end of piece 1; draw a diagonal line.

FIGURE 9 Stitch on the marked line; trim seam to ¼" and press open.

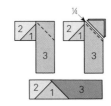

FIGURE 10 Place piece 3 on the right end of the pieced unit; mark, stitch, trim and press.

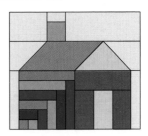

FIGURE 15 Join sections to complete 1 Red Cabin block.

the Red Cabin block with the two X strips referring to the Placement Diagram; press seams toward X.

Step 2. Cut two 1½" x 38½" Y strips and two 1½" x 16½" Z strips tan tone-on-tone. Sew a Y strip to opposite long sides and a Z strip to the top and bottom of the pieced center; press seams toward strips.

Step 3. Join ten Small Log Cabin blocks to make a side row as shown in **Figure 19**; press seams in one direction. Repeat for two side rows. Sew a side row to opposite long sides of the pieced center; press seams toward Y strips.

Step 4. Join six Small Log Cabin blocks to make a top row referring to the Placement Diagram for block positioning; repeat for bottom row. Press seams in one direction. Sew a row to the top and bottom of the pieced center; press seams toward Z strips to complete the pieced top.

Finishing the Quilt

Step 1. Prepare quilt top for quilting and quilt.

Step 2. When quilting is complete, trim batting and backing edges even with the quilted top.

Step 3. Prepare 4½ yards red/blue print binding and bind edges of quilt to finish.

PATRIOTIC CABINS Placement Diagram 24" x 48"

 FIGURE 16 Stitch on the marked line; trim ¼" from stitched line and press open to make triangle/square block centers.

 FIGURE 17 Place a triangle/square right side up on the center of 1 muslin square with red half pointing toward the upper left corner.

FIGURE 19 Join 10 Small Log Cabin blocks to make a side row.

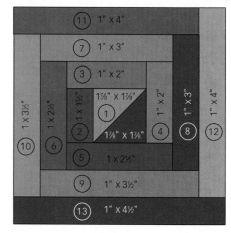

FIGURE 18 Cut pieces in sizes and colors as marked; stitch to center triangle/square unit in numerical order.

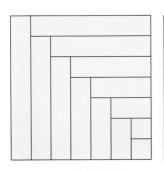

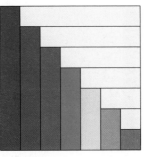

PALE BLUE LOG CABIN

10½" x 10½" Block

MULTICOLORED LOG CABIN

10½" x 10½" Block

DESIGN > LUCY A. FAZELY

Peaceful Journey

Half Log-Cabin blocks create the ship design
in this pieced picture quilt.

PROJECT SPECIFICATIONS

Skill Level: Beginner

Quilt Size: 62½" x 72½"

Block Size: 10½" x 10½"

Number of Blocks 25

MATERIALS

*Note: All fabrics are tone-on-tones and are referred to by
color only in the list of materials and instructions.*

- ⅛ yard each orange and yellow
- ⅙ yard green
- ¼ yard purple
- ¾ yard red
- 1 yard royal blue
- 1⅔ yards pale blue
- 2⅛ yards navy blue
- Backing 69" x 79"
- Batting 69" x 79"
- Neutral color all-purpose thread
- Quilting thread
- Basic sewing tools and supplies

INSTRUCTIONS

Step 1. Cut the following 2" by fabric-width
strips: one each yellow and orange, two each
navy and green, three purple, 11 red, 15 royal
blue, and 27 pale blue.

Step 2. Cut one royal blue, two red and two
pale blue strips into two
equal lengths to yield two
21"–22" strips from each.
Sew the half-strips with
right sides together along
length as follows: one pale
blue/pale blue; one pale
blue/red; one red/red; and
one royal blue/royal blue.

Step 3. Subcut strip sets
into 2" segments as shown

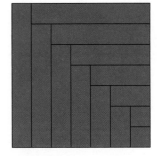

ROYAL BLUE LOG CABIN

10½" x 10½" Block

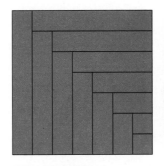

RED LOG CABIN

10½" x 10½" Block

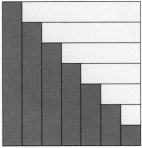

RED/PALE BLUE LOG CABIN

10½" x 10½" Block

in **Figure 1**.

Step 4. Referring to **Figure 2** and pages 9–11 for instructions, sew the 2" segments from Step 3 to 2"-wide colored strips in numerical order to complete the required number of each color block.

Step 5. When blocks are complete, measure and trim to 11" x 11".

Step 6. Arrange blocks in five rows of five blocks each referring to the Placement Diagram for positioning of blocks; press seams in adjoining rows in opposite directions.

Step 7. Join rows to complete the pieced center; press seams in one direction.

Step 8. Cut and piece two 5½" x 53" A strips and two 10½" x 63" B strips navy blue. Sew the A strips to opposite sides and the B strips to the top and bottom of the pieced center; press seams toward strips.

Step 9. Prepare quilt top for quilting and quilt.

Step 10. When quilting is complete, trim batting and backing edges even with the quilted top.

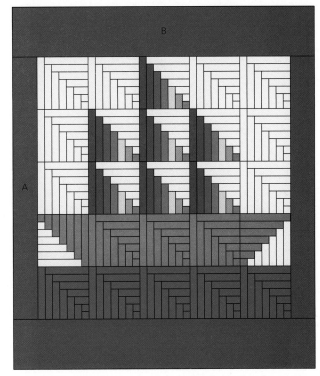

PEACEFUL JOURNEY Placement Diagram 62½" x 72½"

Step 11. Prepare 8½ yards navy blue binding and bind edges of quilt to finish. 🏠

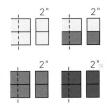

FIGURE 1 Subcut strip sets into 2" segments as shown.

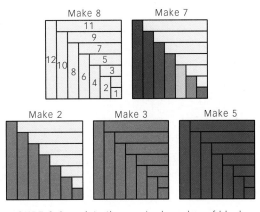

FIGURE 2 Complete the required number of blocks, adding strips in numerical order as shown.

DESIGN > HOLLY DANIELS

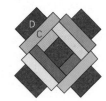

STAINED GLASS DIAMOND
12" x 12" Block

Stained Glass
Diamonds

Black solid strips create the stained glass look
in this simple quilt made with easy pieced blocks
in jewel-tone colors.

PROJECT SPECIFICATIONS

Skill Level: Beginner

Quilt Size: 72" x 84"

Block Size: 12" x 12"

Number of Blocks: 42

MATERIALS

- 5 yards total 12–20 jewel-tone solids, tone-on-tones
  or mottleds
- 5¼ yards black solid
- Backing 78" x 90"
- Batting 78" x 90"
- Neutral color all-purpose thread
- Quilting thread
- Basic sewing tools and supplies

INSTRUCTIONS

Making Blocks

Step 1. Cut four 3½" by fabric width strips
black solid; cut strips into 3½" segments for X.
You will need 42 X squares.

Step 2. Cut 75 strips black solid 2" by fabric
width; subcut strips to make 168 segments
each in the following sizes: 3½" for D; 10½"

for E and 4½" for G.

Step 3. Cut 2" by fabric width strips from jewel-tone fabrics and cut to make 84 segments
each in the following sizes: 3½" for A and 6½"
for B. Cut remaining strips as follows to make
168 segments each in the following sizes: 6½"
for C and 6½" for F.

Step 4. To piece one Stained Glass Diamond
block, stitch any color A piece to opposite
sides of X as shown in **Figure 1**; press seams
away from X.

Step 5. Sew any color B piece to opposite
sides of the A-X unit; press seams toward B.

Step 6. Add any color C piece to opposite
sides of the A-X-B unit; press seams toward C.

Step 7. Add D to opposite sides of the pieced
unit by centering D on C
and sewing as shown in

FIGURE 1 Stitch any
color A piece to
opposite sides of X.

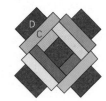

FIGURE 2 Center
and sew D to C.

Figure 2. Trim block to measure 10½" x 10½" as shown in **Figure 3**.

Step 8. Sew pieces E, F and G together, matching centers of pieces as shown in **Figure 4**; repeat for four units. Press seams toward G.

Step 9. Sew one E-F-G unit to each side of the pieced unit as shown in **Figure 5**; press seams away from pieced center.

Step 10. Trim pieced block to 12½" x 12½" as shown in **Figure 6**; repeat for 42 blocks.

Completing the Top

Step 1. Arrange blocks in seven rows of six blocks each; join blocks in rows. Press seams in one direction.

Step 2. Join the rows, alternating directions of seam allowances, to complete the pieced top.

Finishing the Quilt

Step 1. Prepare quilt top for quilting and quilt.

Step 2. When quilting is complete, trim batting and backing edges even with the quilted top.

Step 3. Prepare 9 yards black solid binding and bind edges of quilt to finish. 🏠

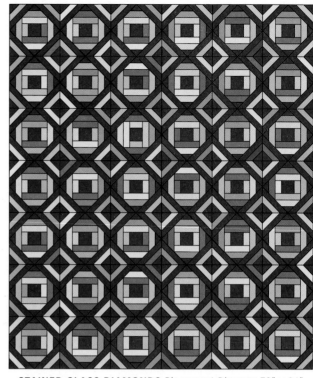

STAINED GLASS DIAMONDS Placement Diagram 72" x 84"

FIGURE 5 Sew 1 E-F-G unit to each side of the pieced unit.

FIGURE 3 Trim block to measure 10½" x 10½".

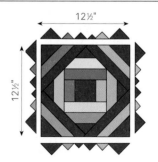

FIGURE 6 Trim pieced block to 12½" x 12½".

FIGURE 4 Sew pieces E, F and G together, matching centers of pieces.

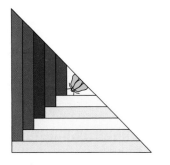

HALF-LOG CABIN REVERSED
9½" x 9½" x 13⅜" Block

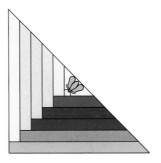

HALF-LOG CABIN
9½" x 9½" x 13⅜" Block

Silk Jewels

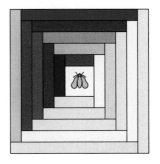

LOG CABIN
9½" x 9½" Block

Silks in rich jewel tones lend a shimmery elegance to the Log Cabin blocks used in this runner with an Oriental flair.

PROJECT NOTES

The sample runner uses fat quarters of Dupioni silk. If you have never worked with silk before, you will find it as strong as cotton, but it frays very easily. Log-Cabin piecing lends itself to foundation piecing, and the reversible nature of the silk makes sewing a breeze. Use a light muslin for the foundations instead of paper to add stability to the completed blocks. Note that the fabric used for the block centers has a gold embroidered insect.

PROJECT SPECIFICATIONS

Skill Level: Beginner
Quilt Size: 57" x 19"
Block Size: 9½" x 9½"
Number of Blocks: 8 and 4 half blocks

MATERIALS

- 6–8 fat quarters dark-value silks—forest green, aqua, royal blue, mulberry, crimson, gold and purple
- 6–8 fat quarters light-value silks—white, cream, pale pink, pale green, silver and beige

- ¼ yard print silk upholstery or other fabric with a 1"-square motif to fit in the block centers (motifs must be at least 2" apart to allow for seam allowance)
- ⅓ yard multicolored silk for binding
- 1 yard lightweight muslin for foundation squares and triangles
- Backing 63" x 25"
- Neutral color all-purpose thread
- Quilting thread
- Basic sewing tools and supplies

INSTRUCTIONS

Step 1. Copy four each A and B foundation patterns.

Step 2. Join one of each to make the Half-Log Cabin design as shown in **Figure 1**; add a ¼" seam allowance to the long edge. Repeat for a Half-Log Cabin Reversed pattern.

Step 3. Join two each A and B patterns to make the Log Cabin pattern, extending log lines as shown in red in **Figure 2**.

Step 4. Mark patterns with numbers for piecing order, and with D and L for dark and light

value placement as shown in **Figure 3**.

Step 5. Cut 10 muslin foundation squares 11" x 11" for Log Cabin blocks. Cut two squares on one diagonal to make two each Half-Log Cabin and Half-Log Cabin Reversed foundations.

Step 6. Transfer lines and numbers from paper patterns to muslin foundations. Trim foundations to exact size on outside marked lines.

Step 7. Cut eight 2½" x 2½" squares print upholstery fabric, centering a motif in each square.

Step 8. Cut 1½"-wide strips from light and dark silks.

Step 9. Place a square right side up on the unmarked side of a muslin foundation square; hold up to a light source to check positioning. Select a dark silk strip; cut a length that extends ¼"–½" beyond the marked area for piece 2 on the foundation and check positioning. Pin in place and stitch on the marked side of the foundation square referring to page 6–8 for instructions.

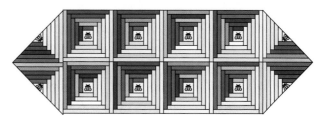

SILK JEWELS Placement Diagram 57" x 19"

Step 10. Continue to add strips around the center on the muslin foundation, again referring to page 6–8 for instructions until the block is complete; repeat for eight Log Cabin blocks.

Step 11. Cut four 3" x 3" squares print upholstery fabric, positioning the motif in one diagonal corner of each square. Complete two Half-Log Cabin blocks and two Half-Log Cabin Reversed blocks using the muslin triangle foundation pieces and referring to the block drawings for positioning of piece 1 motifs and light and dark strips.

Completing the Top

Step 1. Join four Log Cabin blocks to make a row as shown in **Figure 4**; press seams in one

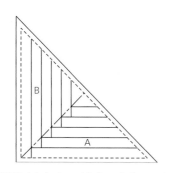

FIGURE 1 Join A and B foundation patterns to make the Half-Log Cabin design; add seam allowance to the long edge.

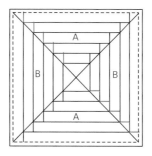

FIGURE 2 Join 2 each A and B patterns and extend log lines shown in red to make the Log Cabin design.

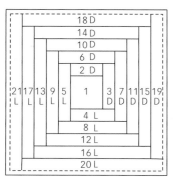

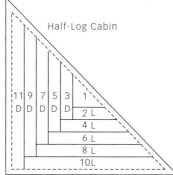

Half-Log Cabin

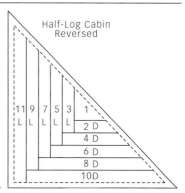

Half-Log Cabin Reversed

FIGURE 3 Mark for piecing order and value placement.

LOG CABIN FOUNDATION PATTERN A

Make 4 copies